COUGAR CONVERTS

Life-Changing Stories from BYU Athletics

Talo Steves, Jedd Parkinson & Matt Hodge

To the remarkable athletes who shared their personal stories with us, and to the thousands of readers and subscribers who have supported Total Blue Sports since 2002

CONTENTS

PREFACE

When we launched Total Blue Sports in 2002, our primary goal was to cover BYU athletics from a different angle than the existing media outlets at the time. Like everyone else, we covered the Cougars' performance on the field and on the court, but we felt that the most compelling aspects of BYU sports were often the personal stories of the athletes.

Approaching our work with that perspective, our coverage was unique, and we soon had hundreds and eventually thousands of loyal subscribers and followers. Of the countless articles we have published over the past decade, the most popular pieces by far have been those that told the stories of BYU athletes away from the field or court of play.

Many of the athletes that have been most beloved by BYU fans were not members of the LDS Church. It takes a unique type of young man to come to BYU as a non-member given the university's honor code and stated mission. These young men with non-LDS backgrounds offer a wonderful perspective and contribution to both the school and BYU sports. In some cases, those athletes gained more than an athletic career and an education during their time in Provo, they also found the gospel of Jesus Christ.

Unfortunately, our website and magazine do not always offer an effective medium for sharing what we feel are some of the best stories we have uncovered along these lines. With that in mind, we decided to publish some of them in book form. We hope you will enjoy reading these stories as much as we enjoyed writing them.

SCOTT COLLIE

The Collie name is synonymous with Brigham Young University football. Scott Collie began the family legacy at BYU, catching balls from future College Football Hall of Fame quarterbacks Marc Wilson, Jim McMahon and Steve Young from 1979 to 1982. Scott's sons Zachary, Austin and Dylan have since added to the Collie family legacy as wide receivers for the Cougars.

Remove the Collie name and the BYU receiving record book, and the program history in general would look very different. What most Cougar fans may not realize is that without a fateful injury to a wide receiver on the Bellarmine High School football team in 1978, there would be no Collie tradition at BYU.

That injury ended the season of one player, but opened a window of opportunity for Scott Collie. That window of opportunity ultimately resulted in dozens of touchdowns, hundreds of receptions and countless lives touched by the gospel of Jesus Christ.

Scott Alan Collie was born in Concordia, Kansas and raised in Northern California by his parents Richard and Ferne. From an early age it was clear that Scott was a gifted athlete. As his father explained, "I've always loved sports and Scott was a good young athlete with terrific ability.

"To give you an example, the first time Scott went to a track meet at the age of five, I had a business and my wife worked for me so we were busy, and my daughter who was 11 said, 'Well I'll take him to the track meet.'

"So she told the story that Scott's lining up for the hundred-yard dash and she's telling him to pay attention and while she's talking to him, the gun goes off. She says, 'Run Scott, run!'"

In spite of giving all of the other runners a big head start, Scott won the race. Scott's exceptional athletic abilities went beyond pure speed. Young Scott also had an incredible arm. "In age group track at that time they had several events and one of them was the baseball throw," Richard recalled.

"Scott got to the point of instead of throwing with the other kids, he'd just wait until they all took their turn and then he'd throw for whatever distance he had to throw to win it. And he won it. He also set a hundred-yard dash record as a nine-year-old for the nation."

Asked about the key to his son's athletic prowess, Richard said, "He had a tremendous amount of natural ability, but also, I always say that he worked hard. I once heard John Elway's dad say that John was not good by accident. And the fact is he worked hard at it. And that's Scott – he was a hard worker."

The elder Collie attributes the athletic success of his son and his three grandsons to hard work. "Scott learned to work hard and his kids learned the same way," Richard said. "Each one of those kids has a reputation of being a hard worker. And that's the difference, in my opinion, between an athlete that excels and one that is just average."

Richard continued, "The best athlete I've ever seen in my life was a kid in high school when Scott was. He was absolutely the best athlete I've ever seen but he wouldn't work. And consequently he ended up not doing well. So if I say anything about Scott, it's that he always has worked harder than anybody else."

After several years in Redwood City, California, Richard and the family moved to nearby San Jose when Scott was in junior high. Scott then attended an all-male Catholic high school, Bellarmine College Preparatory. As expected, the outstanding athletic ability and the unmatched work ethic that Scott had shown from a young age soon translated to success in high school sports.

During his senior year at Bellarmine, Scott began considering his options for college. Excelling at both baseball and football, he started hearing from college recruiters and soon, scholarship offers were on the table.

"I played baseball," Scott said, "and I was being recruited by Santa Clara University to play baseball there and football as well. Brown and Dartmouth University were also a thought, but I really set my sights on going to Oregon State. Three of my high school buddies and I were going to go up there and go to pre-dental school. Football wasn't even in the cards."

While Collie was a good football player, the talent level at Bellarmine was outstanding. The level of talent limited Collie's opportunities to play on the offensive side of the ball, which was always his preference. Collie explained, "We were one of the top teams. We played in a very competitive league. I was one of the starters on defense, but we were so good that nobody went both ways.

"I was a quarterback all the way up through my junior year and then we had a kid come in that was 6'3" or 6'4" and threw the ball. I was a veer quarterback, I ran the option. I think the longest pass I ever threw was 15 yards."

Collie began the season playing linebacker and safety on defense, and his performance at the new positions began to generate attention from college recruiters. It was then that a fateful injury to one of Bellarmine's wide receivers opened a spot for Scott on offense, beginning a chain of events that would have a tremendous impact on Scott's life and that of his family.

Scott recalled: "We're about three quarters of the way done with the season and I start getting letters. That was kind of interesting. Then I get called down to the coach's office in the middle of class one day. I have no idea what it's for, so I go down there and there was this older-looking gentleman sitting down in a chair."

Scott would soon learn that the "older-looking gentleman" sitting in the chair was legendary BYU offensive coordinator Doug Scovil.

"Our quarterback, Mike Jones, was there and he was already sitting down," Scott said.

"So this Doug Scovil - I didn't know who it was, I had never even heard of Brigham Young University - started telling me and Mike about this program and how they throw the ball all the time. Gifford Nielsen and Marc Wilson, Gary Sheide, and that's all they do is throw the ball, and he wanted us to come up and look at the school.

"I then very politely explained to Doug Scovil that there would be no way that my parents would pay for me to come up and look at a school. And he said, 'No, you don't get it, we're going to fly you up to come look at the school.' And I about peed my pants! I had no idea that anybody would do that!"

Scott couldn't believe what he was hearing from Scovil. "I was completely shocked," Scott said. "I didn't even play varsity football as a junior. I wasn't the best football player on the team. I wasn't the guy who had all the touchdowns. I didn't even start playing receiver until halfway through the season when one of our receivers got hurt. I played defense. I kicked and I punted and I was the back-up quarterback."

So what led to this unexpected opportunity? "Doug Scovil happened to be at a game and saw me catch the ball," Scott said. "The other schools recruiting me saw me play defensive back and linebacker, but I didn't like that. Doug Scovil said, 'I want you to play receiver.' And it fell into place from there."

Scott's father remembers the recruiting process as it unfolded throughout Scott's senior season. "He had numerous colleges talking to him and they'd come to the house," Richard said.

"We'd sit down in the living room with them and quite often they'd have a cup of coffee and then they'd proceed to tell us how good of a football player Scott was going to be. We had several coaches that way and they knew that he was a good kid. But one evening a guy named LaVell Edwards came to our house and he didn't have a cup of coffee."

Declining coffee was just the first indicator that the coach from BYU was a little different than the others who had visited the Collie home. Richard recalled Coach Edwards' famous sense of humor, including a comment he made about Scott during that first visit to their home. "As we sat down and started talking, LaVell said, 'If I had a kid that good looking, I wouldn't let him play football.'"

The head coach from BYU also described a different vision for Scott as a student athlete, a difference noted by Scott's parents. "LaVell then proceeded to tell us that he wanted Scott to come to BYU for an education and for the social life, that he was going to learn and then that he was going to play some football," Richard said. "I said to Scott's mother afterwards, 'Even if he's lying to us, at least he's telling us what we want to hear.' Of course, as it ended up, it was true."

Scott visited some other schools and then took his recruiting visit to BYU and liked what he saw.

"I went ahead and took other recruiting trips," Scott said. "I had this vision that I was going to be a forest ranger. I had

BYU WR Scott Collie   Photo Mark A. Philbrick/BYU

already left my pre-dental plans and thought I want to be a forest ranger, and now being in the mountains of Provo was going to be perfect."

Richard remembers talking to Scott after his recruiting trips to different schools, and how the atmosphere was markedly different from what Scott then saw at BYU. "Then he went to BYU," Richard explained. "He came home, I picked him up at the airport, and he said, 'I'm going to BYU.'"

Upon graduation from Bellarmine, Scott began preparing for the move to Provo, Utah. Scott recalled an experience during that time. "During that summer while getting prepared to go up to BYU, I met a couple kids at some summer parties and they said, 'Oh, are you the guy who's going to BYU?'" Scott confirmed that he was BYU-bound and a girl said, "Oh I'm Mormon, too. I'm going to BYU."

That comment caught Scott a bit off guard. "Of course we were at a party," Scott explained. "I'm sure she was not partaking of anything and I might have been holding a beer and she said, 'And that's not going to work at BYU.'"

That comment and others led Scott to realize that life at BYU would be different from what he had known in San Jose, and he became a bit concerned about some of what he was hearing.

"I started hearing rumors from other people of what it was going to be like at BYU," Scott said. "One specific thing I remember is they told us at midnight they would come down the hallways and knock on your door and you had to come out into the dark hallway and chant with them. So my roommate who was the quarterback, Mike Jones, we both got scholarship offers and we both went to BYU. So we're sitting in our room that first night at about 11:55 and we're ready to pounce on the first person that knocks on our door.

"At about 12:05 we went out into the hallway and nobody was there. So we said, 'Okay, maybe it's tomorrow night.' So we did the same thing the next night and then we realized that maybe that wasn't accurate."

After dispelling the hallway chanting rumor, Mike and Scott began learning more about the Church and its teachings. "We ended up then starting school," Scott said. "We of course had to take the required Book of Mormon class. And as it goes, sometimes you aren't really working hard enough in class or not paying as much attention as you should be, particularly not knowing how important it was.

"So we went through the first semester and started into the second semester and then we got our own place living with Danny Plater and a couple others. Then Mike said, 'You know, if we're going to be here we might as well learn what this thing is about and maybe take a Cliffs Notes course on the Book of Mormon.' And we invited the missionaries over."

Scott still remembers seeing Mike's reaction to the first meeting with the Mormon elders.

"Mike had the discussion the first night and he came out of the room like he had seen a ghost," Scott said with a chuckle. "My night was the second night, and I sat there on the edge of my bed just waiting for this same experience that Mike had, and it wasn't there. So I was quite disappointed in that. I was probably paying more attention to trying to see ghosts than I was listening to the lesson. And when the missionaries concluded, they said, 'We want to teach you to pray. Have you ever prayed before?'"

Collie replied that he had never prayed. "I always played like I was atheist," Scott explained. "And then I knelt down to pray and I was overcome by the Holy Ghost. And it fell into place real quick."

Richard remembers the phone call from Scott explaining that he was planning to join the Church of Jesus Christ of Latter-day Saints. "So one night Scott called me and said I'm going to join the Mormon Church," Richard recalled. "I said Scott, there's nothing more personal or more important than that decision you're making. And I want you to be the best Mormon you can be, but don't bring it home."

In the months immediately following his baptism, Scott had numerous opportunities to share his conversion story.

"When you're baptized and you have an experience like that, that's where your testimony comes from," Scott said. "Being immature, there was a lot of attention that I got because I was a football player, because I was baptized, and so there were opportunities to speak at zone conferences and opportunities to speak at sacrament meetings and firesides. That lasted about six months.

"But what happened at the end of the six months is that I was kind of left to go hang on my own. And then having not a testimony of the gospel per se, or having only a shallow testimony, you don't have anything to really sink your teeth into, and so I began to become lazy and ended up then making some choices and didn't really live the gospel as it should have been at that time."

Thinking back on what led to his struggles during that period, Collie explained, "I didn't think that I could be a Mormon in the sense that I didn't look forward to going to church for three hours on Sunday. And then the idea of I'm going to go to Hell because I have a beer? How can you go to Hell if you have a beer? So I had all of these immature thoughts and I kind of went that way for about a year. And then you know as it goes, I met a girl."

The girl Scott met was Nicole Norman, an LDS co-ed from Sacramento, California. "I can remember on our first date explaining to her that I was a convert to the Church but I wasn't active in the Church, and that if I ever was active in the Church that I wouldn't get married in the temple because I wanted my parents to be there," Scott said. "I dated her for about two months and then I remember about the second month thinking, 'You know, that temple thing, it might not be a bad idea.'"

As his relationship with Nicole grew, Scott also gained a greater understanding of the gospel of Jesus Christ and what it meant to be a member of the Church.

"I began to learn about the gospel," Scott said. "I had an opportunity to meet her parents. I began to understand that the gospel is a relationship with Jesus Christ. You have a priesthood responsibility. You honor that. I began to understand that the gospel and the things within it only bring you happiness.

"And so as I began to understand and truly gain my own testimony, a proper testimony, I still had that experience that I could not deny and that was the Holy Ghost bearing witness to me in that first prayer that this was real. So from then, a year later [in July, 1981] I had an opportunity to be married in the temple. And the rest is history."

Asked about his family's reaction to his conversion and his marriage in the temple, Scott explained that both of his parents were raised in religious homes and were supportive of religion in general.

"My parents were raised with fire and brimstone – you do this, you go to Hell," Scott said. "Growing up, we didn't do a lot of church things. I think we might have gone to Easter Sunday a couple of times, but they were all for BYU. Again, I wasn't Catholic and I went to a Catholic school. They thought, hey, if you get religion, get religion. We believed in a higher power.

"So when it came time for the baptism they were excited. When it came time for the wedding in the temple, my mom was a little bit confused on why she couldn't attend. And I told her she could, here's what you got to do. Anyway, they were accepting of it. Interestingly enough, my sister who was a born-again Christian used to call me and my wife and tell us she was praying for our souls and things we needed to do to have our souls saved."

On the football field, Collie played with BYU quarterback greats Mark Wilson, Jim McMahon and Steve Young. They were part of some of the most potent offenses in BYU history. "What I remember of those teams was the utter dominance that we had with the passing attack," said Collie.

"Back then, it wasn't if we were going to score, it was how we were going to score. It was interesting to see how teams tried to defend against it. One team dropped 10 guys into pass coverage and rushed one. We saw every type of blitz. We saw teams do things, even to the point of trying to get into our heads. One team, I think it may have been UTEP, didn't come out on the field for warm-ups."

After a strong junior season in which he caught 26 passes, scored three touchdowns, and led an extremely talented receiving corps in yards per catch, Collie became a primary option on the Cougar offense his senior season. "I was playing well and I had an invitation to play in the East-West Shrine Game, but I ended up then getting hurt and missed the rest of the season," Collie explained.

In spite of missing much of his senior year, Collie made a strong impression in his limited action and the Denver Gold selected him with the 64th overall pick in the initial USFL draft. Unable to reach a contact agreement with Denver, Collie instead accepted a free-agent offer with his favorite NFL team, the San Francisco 49ers.

"I was one of the last rookies cut, and my claim to fame was that I was cut by Bill Walsh," he said. Players cut early on are often informed by an equipment manager or low-level employee, but Collie was cut by "the head guy." One week later, Collie joined the Hamilton Tiger Cats of the Canadian Football League, where he would play for the next four years.

While he made a big impact as an athlete at BYU and then in professional football, Scott's greatest impact has been off the field.

BYU WR Dylan Collie   Photo Troy Verde/Total Blue

In addition to a successful career as an executive providing technology solutions in the hospitality industry, Scott found time to coach his three sons, along with hundreds of other young athletes over the years.

While the Collie boys were great athletes on the field, what separated them in the eyes of many coaches and media members was their behavior and demeanor off the field.

"It's been interesting," Scott said. "When Dylan made the verbal commitment to go to BYU, my wife and I got a number of calls from those, I'm sure of the LDS faith, from around the country and it was that question: 'What did you do? You've got three boys now who have been able to go up through junior football, high school football, and now play Division I football. You had a daughter [Taylore] who was able to get a golf scholarship to play golf at Utah Valley University. What are you doing as parents?'"

In response to these inquiries, Scott would explain that while he didn't necessarily give parental advice, he could help them coach their children. "There is so much parallel between football and real life that quite often parenting comes out in the coaching," Scott said.

The numerous requests he received for private coaching sessions eventually motivated Scott to leave his career and pursue his dream of coaching football full-time. In 2012, Scott launched ReceiverTech and began offering specialized training, camps and competitions to help young players maximize their potential.

Collie shared some of the philosophy that he and his wife used in raising children. "There wasn't a privileged child in the house. Quite often in a home where you have a superior athlete, the entire home becomes focused on that one child. That wasn't allowed in our home.

"It didn't matter if someone was going to a debate, if someone was going to sing at church, it didn't matter. Their event was just

BYU WR Zac Collie   Photo ReceiverTech

as important as the next person's. I think sometimes parents begin to lean toward the individual child who maybe has an opportunity, where they're going to that one child's tournaments, but there wasn't anyone left behind in our home. And that was a credit to my wife."

The gospel played a central role in the way the Collies raised their children. "We were disciplinarians. We were consistent. We put the gospel first. And granted, a lot of people would probably shake their head at some of the things we do in our home, but it worked for the Collie family."

Scott's gospel-centered approach as a father blessed the lives of his children, and Scott's own father also noticed.

"The only thing I knew about the Church when Scott was going to BYU were families that I knew that were in the Church," said Richard. "I've been in other churches. We went to church and I belonged to the Baptist Church and I was a member of the Presbyterian Church. But the difference I saw in The Church of Jesus Christ of Latter-day Saints, there it's a seven-day-a-week religion."

In watching his son raise his young family, Richard also noticed that their lives and the Church they attended were centered on the family. "I discovered with The Church of Jesus Christ of Latter-day Saints that number one, it's a family church. And I've always been a strong family person. And that's what I've seen is that they take care of their families."

Richard's direction to Scott when he decided to join the Church at BYU was to be the best Mormon he could be, but to not force his religious beliefs on the rest of the family.

"Scott did a good job of not trying to preach to me. But the other thing he did, he started raising a family and conducting himself in a way that I wished I would have been that kind of a father. We'd go to Christmas and we'd have a nice church program [with Scott and his family] and I would get tears in my

BYU WR Austin Collie   Photo Troy Verde/Total Blue Sports

eyes because I wished I had been that kind of a father."

While Scott's parents were supportive of his decision to join the Church and raise his family according to its principles, his older sister was not. "I told Scott not to bring that religion home, but the first thing I know, my daughter's giving him a bad time about it," Richard recalled.

"My daughter Debbie did not support him in being baptized. She was in what I would call a Bible church and she was listening to a preacher who didn't know what he was talking about. He was talking about it being a cult, that the Mormons didn't believe in Jesus Christ, and the stuff that people that don't understand the Church sometimes talk about.

"Like today, it's true ignorance when people start talking about this Church because they don't know what they're talking about. I tell people today, if people don't believe in the Church, it's through ignorance. And ignorance is not being dumb, it's just not being aware of the facts."

Over time, Scott's example began to outweigh the ideas that his sister Debbie had been led to believe with regards to the Church. "Debbie learned about the Church by watching Scott and it opened the mind and she ended up being baptized," Richard said. Not long after her baptism, Debbie and the rest of the Collie family received some terrible news.

"Shortly after joining the Church my sister was diagnosed with cancer and then died just short of her opportunity to go through the temple," Scott explained. "She had prepared hard and fast to go to the temple but she had passed away before."

Within a short period of Debbie's passing, Richard followed his daughter and son into the waters of baptism. He described his conversion, a process which spanned over two decades.

"For us in the Church, we often get people by attraction rather than promotion. And that's exactly what happened to me. I watched Scott with his family, his wife, his kids and his in-laws,

Austin, Scott, Dylan and Zac Collie   Photos Receivertech

and I wanted what they had. So after several years of procrastination I joined the Church. I never made a better decision in all my life. So today we're one big happy family that's going to live [together] forever."

While he delayed his decision to join the Church for many years, Richard is open about the blessings that decision has brought him. His excitement about the gospel is impossible to hide and he loves to talk about the Church. "My dad is absolutely is a typical convert," Scott said. "That's all he wants to talk about!"

As Richard reflects on the blessings he has enjoyed because of the gospel, he is grateful that the BYU coaches saw Scott catch the ball back in 1978 and then recruited him to play receiver for the Cougars. The elder Collie has fond memories of his association with the BYU football program, and it all began with Coach Edwards visiting his home so many years ago.

"If I had a kid today and I wanted to send him away for the first time in his life, I'd pick LaVell Edwards. And when I say LaVell I include [his wife] Patti also because Patti and LaVell, you couldn't send your kid to better people than to them," Richard said.

"I feel the same way about Coach Bronco Mendenhall. Bronco has restored the prestige and the honor in Brigham Young University. Austin and Dylan had other people recruiting them, but they went to BYU. And when they have kids, I bet you they go to BYU."

Richard has had the opportunity to watch his son and then his grandsons excel in college football and then go on to play professionally, Scott in the CFL and both Zac and Austin in the NFL. While millions of fathers dream of that opportunity, Richard has a unique perspective on the accomplishments of his son and grandsons.

"I watched Scott one day at the University of Georgia score a couple of touchdowns," Richard said. "I've watched Scott make some other good catches, but the proudest I've ever been was when I listened to Scott give a talk in church.

"Just a few weeks ago I was in Sacramento and I went to one of his football camps. Scott knows football and he's able to communicate it to these kids, but it's more important than football. If one of those boys ... or if 10 of them ... become great NFL players, then great, but if they don't, they're still getting a good lesson about life and love from the way Scott handles those kids.

"And Austin is the same way. When Austin scores a touchdown, yeah, I'm grateful he scores a touchdown. But I'm more grateful when Austin tells me about a kid who was doing this or that on the Colts and they say, 'Well what would Austin Collie do?' Austin, when he's interviewed, will never deny the Church. He always in some way or another gets the word in about the Church.

"So long after each one of these kids quits playing football, they're still going to have the Church and a beautiful family. And again, I love football, and I love to watch Austin and Dylan and Zac play. But what they have and what they've learned at home is far more important than football. And it's not just Scott. Nicki is a great mother. Nicki is a person that...those kids and Scott come first every time with her. Needless to say, I'm real grateful."

Reflecting on his decisions to play football at BYU and to join the Church as a freshman in Provo, Scott realizes that the impact those choices had surpasses anything he ever imagined.

"It's kind of interesting to see that from that one baptism, two sons [served missions] and then a third one [is] getting prepared to go on a mission. To see what they have, and what missionaries can do to change lives and directions all for the better, to watch my sons go out and have an opportunity to serve and introduce families to the gospel and individuals to the gospel, just as it was to me, and then to start that whole thing all over again, it's an exciting thing."

2

CURTIS BROWN

The 2002 BYU football recruiting class was widely considered the best in school history, at least on paper. Even after the last-minute defection of five-star defensive tackle Haloti Ngata to Oregon, the class still included three five-star recruits and three four-star recruits. Expectations were high, but the next few years would demonstrate that recruiting is an inexact science and star ratings don't always translate to impact on the field.

Ben Olson, the nation's top quarterback recruit who headlined the class, would redshirt as a freshman, serve a mission to Canada and then transfer to UCLA, where his career never matched his immense hype due to injuries and ineffectiveness. Walt Williams, a five-star, all-world junior college cornerback, signed but never enrolled at BYU or anywhere else and remains an internet legend and man of mystery to this day. Scott Young, a five-star defensive tackle out of Dixie College, did contribute, but did so after being switched to the offensive line his senior season. Like Young, four-star defensive tackle signee Jake Kuresa was also moved from defensive tackle to the offensive line, where he became a solid four-year starter for the Cougars. Four-star junior college safety Chad Barney, also from Dixie College, became a starter for the

Cougars but was never a game-changer at the Division I level. Mulivai Pula, the explosive running back out of Hawaii's Kahuku High School who looked like the second coming of Luke Staley on film, eventually enrolled at Dixie College due to academics and never made it back to BYU.

Fortunately for BYU fans, four other players from the 2002 signee list made a tremendous impact on the program in spite of being some of the lowest-rated recruits of the class. Two-star linebacker Bryan Kehl and unranked players Fui Vakapuna, Andrew George and Curtis Brown would become household names to BYU fans in spite of receiving limited attention from the national recruiting services. All four players excelled on the field, but Brown arguably made the greatest impact of the four.

A native of Palmdale, California, Brown was unknown to all but the most ardent fans when he signed with the Cougars on February 6, 2002. Although Brown rushed for an astounding 7,045 career yards for Paraclete High School, Gary Crowton and the BYU staff didn't begin to pursue him in earnest until late in the recruiting season. In spite of the limited early recruiting attention, Brown signed with BYU and made his mark on the field, eventually leaving BYU as the school's career rushing leader with 3,193 yards. He also finished with 34 touchdowns and a school-record 15 100-yard rushing games to his credit.

Football stardom didn't arrive overnight for Brown. Like most freshmen, he was used sparingly during his first year of Division I football, but in the fifth week of the season against Utah State, Brown gave Cougar fans a preview of what was to come. Brown broke onto the scene that day, leading a BYU comeback that erased a 34-7 halftime deficit as the Cougars pulled out a 35-34 win on the road in Logan. The true freshman finished the day with 217 yards rushing and three touchdowns, adding another 49 yards on four receptions.

As he began preparing for his sophomore season, Brown was

BYU RB Curtis Brown   Photo Troy Verde/Total Blue Sports

disappointed to learn that the coaches planned to redshirt him in 2003. He had been anxious to improve on his solid freshman performance, but the redshirt year became an important time of introspection and personal growth. "I was just trying to figure out life in general," Brown explained. "Obviously coming to BYU, I had high expectations as far as football was concerned, then having to redshirt...I realized there was more to life than football."

During the redshirt season, Curtis was sharing an apartment with LDS teammates Corby Hodgkiss and Kellen Fowler, and he often found himself alone on Sundays. "It seemed like on Sundays I would be by myself in the apartment. They'd take off and go to church and then they'd come back and they'd be joking about what happened at church, or they'd break the fast or whatever. They'd have dinner over at this girl's house and I'm like, 'I feel left out.'" Teammate Matt Berry eventually invited him to attend church with him one Sunday, and Brown was overwhelmed by how welcome and loved he felt in spite of having just met most of those in attendance.

Wanting to learn more about the Church, Brown decided to talk to long-time BYU athletic trainer George Curtis. "George Curtis had always been on my case about investigating the Church and he said I seemed like a bright guy that he'd love to take under his wing," Brown said. "I decided one day I wanted to learn more and I felt like George was the guy to go to because he'd keep it private and it was something that I could discover for myself and not have any other outside influences. So one day I went up to him after football practice and said, 'Hey, I'd like to learn more,' and he set it up to meet with the missionaries. I went through the discussions and eight, 10 weeks later I was getting dunked under the water."

Asked about the conversion process that took place over those weeks, Curtis remembered a lot of prayers along with some

Photo Troy Verde/Total Blue Sports

struggles. "It's interesting," Brown said. "I don't know if other people go through this, but it was more like it was revealed to me that it wasn't not true. After every discussion they asked us to go home and pray about it, to pray to know if this gospel is true. I'd go home and I'd pray really hard and I'd read the scriptures they had me read. I'd sit there and at the end of the day I'm praying and I'm thinking is this true or is this not true, or give me a sign. And then at the end of it...after receiving the discussions, I hadn't received anything negative but I hadn't received anything telling me that it is true."

Like many investigators before him, Brown was expecting the answer to come in a different form than it actually came. "I felt like everything was going well and I felt happy about it, but I was waiting more for Him to appear in a dream or something like that. So, the night before I was supposed to get baptized I called up Matt Berry and I said, 'Hey Matt, I'm having some cold feet.' So he comes and he picks me up and we go over and park in front of the Provo temple. It's like 9:30 at night and I'm...uh...parking in front of the temple. This is pretty interesting," Brown said with a chuckle.

Brown said he and Berry sat in the car quietly for about 10 minutes until his teammate finally broke the silence, explaining that this was a place he would go when he wanted to be alone and needed answers from his Heavenly Father. Berry asked Brown what his biggest fears were about joining the Church. "I said my ultimate thing is that this is a big decision and I want it to be the right one and I would hate to go through this process, get baptized and find out a couple of weeks later it's not true and to have that regret," Brown said. "He just told me that ultimately his personal opinion was that the Church is true and he said that this gospel is so simple that anyone on this earth can comprehend it, but it's so complex that only the strongest of men can make it through and be successful. Ultimately I took that as it's

Photo Troy Verde/Total Blue Sports

something that is easy to understand but it's harder to live.

"He said you're never going to have all the answers. There's going to be things that you're going to continue to question. He said he's been a member his whole life and there's still things that he still has questions about. He said ultimately Heavenly Father will tell you if you're making the wrong decision and if he hasn't given you any negative feelings so far, then go with that. That's when I realized that sometimes Heavenly Father is not necessarily there to tell us everything, whether it's right or wrong. When we're doing something good he's going to continue to give us those positive feelings and that's what I felt. I just felt that positive emotion over me every day. Every day I had an opportunity to meet with the missionaries and interact with teammates of the LDS faith, it was a positive experience. To this day I still have those experiences. I'll never deny the gospel because I know that I've felt so positive about life since I entered into that covenant with Heavenly Father."

On February 21, 2004, Brown was baptized a member of the Church by Berry. Leading up to that day, Brown was unsure how he should handle the situation with regards to his family. "At first I didn't even want to tell my family that I was getting baptized because I felt like it's personal, I don't need to bug them with it," Brown explained. "I wasn't sure how they'd respond." He ultimately decided to tell them about his plans and invited them to attend the ceremony in Provo. Two days after attending her son's baptismal service, Cheryl Brown penned an article on TotalBlueSports.com describing the experience from her unique perspective as a mother and a member of another faith.

"My son Curtis Brown, a running back on the BYU football team, was baptized and confirmed a member of The Church of Jesus Christ of Latter-day Saints last Saturday in Provo," she wrote. "His father, brother, sister and I are not LDS members, but we were thrilled with his decision and would not have missed it

Photo Troy Verde/Total Blue Sports

for the world. I can honestly say I saw it coming for some time and was not too surprised. I have witnessed and marveled at the growth and maturity in my son since he has been at BYU. As parents, how can we not be proud and supportive when our adult child chooses to accept God as his Savior and commits to live his life in accordance with God's word.

"I truly appreciate the love and support my son has received from so many in the BYU community. Be assured as members of The Church of Jesus Christ of Latter-day Saints, the Gospel is moving forward at BYU and lives are being changed, one at a time. I would personally like to thank Matt Berry, a BYU quarterback, and George Curtis, the BYU trainer, for the spiritual guidance they provided Curtis and being there for him on a daily basis. In addition, I would like to thank the many BYU coaches, athletic department staff members, his teammates and friends who led by example and were such a positive influence in my son's life. As parents, we are ever mindful that our actions speak louder than words.

"Since our affiliation with this unique and special university, the BYU coaches and supporting staff have done nothing but conduct themselves with integrity and dignity. For that, we are forever grateful. The male athletes at BYU are blessed to have them as role models since they are our future fathers, husbands, church leaders, community activists, etc. Thank you Bishop Edgley, a member of the LDS Church's Presiding Bishopric, for taking time out from your busy schedule to participate at this joyous occasion. How profound your words were when you assured Curtis that, as the newest member of the Church, that it is as much his to claim as it is yours.

"When Curtis told us he wanted to be baptized into the LDS Church, I never once felt that I was losing a son, but gaining a whole new family. This fact has been amplified in my mind and with members of my family over and over since Saturday. Thank you all for the kind words and best wishes. I will be sure to pass them along to Curtis."[1]

More than 150 people were in attendance that day as Curtis Brown began a new chapter in his life. Looking back on the experience nearly a decade later, he is grateful for the love and support he received from his family and friends. "Knowing that they were there supporting me, having quite a few people there supporting me, I didn't realize at the time how big of a deal it was," he said. "To see the kind of support I got from friends and family was a pretty awesome experience and it's something I'll take with me for the rest of my life."

Within weeks of his baptism, Brown was back on the field for spring football as the team began preparing for the 2004 season. After redshirting the previous season and going through his conversion process off the field, Brown was anxious to get back on the gridiron with his teammates. Brown had a solid spring performance and followed it with a strong fall camp and was rewarded with a substantial increase in playing time as a sophomore. He split time at running back with future NFL back Fahu Tahi, starting six games on the season and leading the team with 789 yards rushing. He averaged five yards per carry and scored six touchdowns. Brown also showed his versatility by catching 27 passes and throwing a 40-yard touchdown pass to Austin Collie against Wyoming. The sophomore was recognized for his outstanding play by being named to the All-Mountain West Conference second team.

Those close to the program knew that Brown was poised for a breakout season, and that breakout came in 2005. He started every game as a junior and rushed for 1,123 yards, scored 16 touchdowns and caught 53 passes for nearly 500 yards. Brown was named first-team All-Mountain West Conference. He combined with fellow All-Conference performers John Beck and Johnny Harline to lead a potent Cougar offense that averaged 33

Touchdown!   Photo Troy Verde/Total Blue Sports

points a game for the season.

As he began his final season in Provo, Brown was approaching the all-time Cougar rushing record held by Jamal Willis. The running back who received little fanfare upon signing with BYU was now in a position to finish his career as the most productive running back in school history. Brown did not disappoint. He delivered another thousand-yard rushing season in 2006 and added 62 receptions for 566 yards, making him the all-time BYU record-holder for both career rushing yards and all-purpose yards. These accomplishments also put Brown in very select company on a national level. He remains one of only 24 players in FBS college football history to have at least 3,000 career rushing yards and 1,000 receiving yards, an honor he shares with former BYU running back Harvey Unga.

Brown, Beck and Harline were once again key cogs in a powerful Cougar offense that averaged 36.7 points a game in 2006. The trio of seniors led the team to an 11-2 season that was capped off by a 38-8 drubbing of the Oregon Ducks in the Las Vegas Bowl. Brown finished his career on a high note, rushing for 120 yards on just 17 carries while scoring two touchdowns in the bowl victory.

Brown has many great memories from his record-breaking career as a Cougar running back, but his fondest BYU memory occurred away from the football field. "I found my eternal companion, my wife Kimberly," Brown said with a grin. "I've been married – it will be six years in August [2012]. We got married in the Oakland temple."

Brown shared his testimony of the gospel, describing the foundation of his faith, the gratitude he feels and what inspires him to be an example to others. "I know the Church is true," he said. "I know that Heavenly Father revealed the truth to Joseph Smith and let him know that this was the true church. I'm so thankful for this gospel in my life and the opportunities it's

Photo Troy Verde/Total Blue Sports

blessed me with. One of the things I always tell people who are interested in learning about the Church but are kind of skeptical about things, ultimately what it comes down to is Heavenly Father wants us to be representatives of what He stands for. I felt like the LDS Church is the best church amongst any of those churches on this earth. It does the best job of representing Him with charity, with selfless acts, with the representation of its members and the high standards that we hold. I feel like if Heavenly Father were to step on this earth today, He would say, 'You guys are representing me well.' I take pride in that. I take pride in being part of this gospel and I'm grateful for all the blessings and the things that I've been blessed with as part of this Church."

3

TOM HOLMOE

Late in his senior season at Crescenta Valley High School in California, star quarterback Tom Holmoe took a beating in a game, suffering an injury to a finger on his throwing hand and a ruptured elbow bursa. Holmoe was looking forward to the league championship game the following week and figured the injuries were just another minor bump in the road on the way to the playoffs.

"I'm at a friend's house that night," Holmoe said while reflecting on the incident. "I've got ice on my elbow and my hand hurts. The next day my finger was swollen and my dad said, 'I'm going to take you to the doctor, you've got to get that X-rayed.'" When Holmoe and his father arrived at the emergency room, Dr. Brent Pratley was the attending physician. After an anxious wait, "You're done" was the blunt diagnosis from Pratley, definitely not what Holmoe wanted to hear. The X-ray revealed a shattered finger on his throwing hand, a detail that seemed irrelevant to the young quarterback at the time.

"I said the championship game for the league is next week," Holmoe recalled, to which Dr. Pratley again responded, "You're done." Holmoe assured the doctor that the finger was fine, telling him that he could just tape it up and play. "No you're not," Pratley said. "You're going to play college football and you're going to be a star, but you're not going to play another game this year until we fix that."

Holmoe left the hospital, devastated by the news that his high school football career was over. He sadly informed his coach of the doctor's diagnosis and the surgery that was planned. Knowing all too well that losing his starting quarterback would severely hamper the team's playoff hopes, the coach suggested Holmoe skip the surgery and play anyway. Although he agreed with his coach's sentiments and wanted desperately to play in the championship game, Holmoe knew he couldn't. He regretfully informed the coach, "I'm done. I can't play. I have to have surgery next week."

A gifted young quarterback, Holmoe stood at 6 feet 3 inches and possessed a rare combination of size and speed. He was being heavily recruited by a number of top colleges, including the University of Oregon, Brigham Young University and Washington State. However, the interest level for many of the schools waned after they learned of the serious injury to the finger on his throwing hand. Not only had the injury ended his season, it had also damaged his prospects of playing quarterback in college. "So I had surgery, missed the last game, missed the playoffs, and a lot of teams dropped me at that time." Holmoe recalled.

Holmoe still took recruiting trips to several schools, but the injury remained a concern, even for the schools that were still interested. "I had to have it pinned and wired and I had a ball on my hand during all the recruiting visits," Holmoe said. "So people wondered, 'What's wrong with this guy? Is he going to be okay? He broke his hand.'"

BYU was one of the schools that continued to aggressively

recruit Holmoe in spite of the injury, but Holmoe saw a logjam at quarterback at the school from Provo. "I really wasn't that interested in BYU until after I got hurt," Holmoe recalled. "They had Marc Wilson and Jim McMahon. Then they said, 'You know what, we like you as a defensive back too.'

"LaVell [Edwards] and Dick Felt and Fred Whittingham recruited me. They did a really good job and the team was good. I did research and the academics were really good and I was a good student. So they brought me up [to Provo] on a trip and that's where it started. I met the players and I went to the Marriott Center and saw a game where Danny Ainge was playing against Utah State and it was full to the brim. I'm like, 'Wow, this is something!' I felt the Spirit. I didn't know it at the time, but there was an incredible spirit. When I flew home on the flight that next day I knew that I liked this place."

Holmoe accepted the idea of playing defense instead of offense at the college level, and the more he compared BYU with the other options available to him, the more he liked the idea of going to school and playing football in Provo. However, BYU was not a popular choice among his friends and family. "I went on a couple other trips after that, and every time people would go, 'Oh, you'll like it better than BYU,'" Holmoe said. "And every time I'm flying home I'm thinking no, I like BYU best. When it was all said and done everybody wanted me to go somewhere else, but I was the only one who wanted me to go to BYU. My family didn't want me to go to there, my friends didn't want me to go there, my coaches didn't want me to go there, nobody. All the negative recruiting, it was a lot tougher back then that it is now. Every coach was tearing up BYU and still it was like, 'This is the place for you, you got to go.'"

In spite of the negative comments he was hearing about BYU and the Mormon church that sponsored it, Holmoe had developed a different perspective over the years. "I had a couple of friends that were LDS. They're still my friends and they were different. They stood out. The Hales family, Klane was a year older than me and he had a little sister, Kathy, who was a year younger than me, so I was right in between them and we were really good friends. They were really dear friends of mine, so when I got a letter from BYU, the first letter, I'm like, 'BYU?'" Holmoe was intrigued.

"I didn't really know much about the school or the football program," Holmoe recalled. "I think I was a junior and I started early in my junior year to look at BYU and I followed the team a little bit. Giff [Nielsen] was the quarterback and they were good. They were coming on and LaVell was a young head coach. So when they recruited me, I measured what it would possibly be like to be at BYU based on my LDS friends." When others warned him about the perceived negative aspects of attending the religious school with its strict honor code, Holmoe would respond, "Why? These guys are some of my best friends and if it's anything like them, I'd want to go."

Looking beyond the negative pressure he was receiving from all directions, Holmoe followed his heart and committed to play football for Brigham Young University. After arriving on campus in 1978, Holmoe quickly made an impact on the field. He saw regular playing time at defensive back as a true freshman and made a big impact on special teams for a Cougar team that finished the season 11-1 and won the WAC championship. Holmoe followed his solid freshman campaign with a breakout performance as a sophomore. In his first season as a full-time starter, Holmoe was named the coaches' player of the game five times. He led the league in interceptions with seven, totaled 57 tackles and was named to the All-Conference and All-District academic teams. The team finished 12-1, capping off the season with the legendary come-from-behind victory against SMU in the

Holiday Bowl.

Continuing where he left off the prior year, Holmoe had another great season as a junior. The Cougars were once again very strong, finishing the season 11-2 with a victory over Washington State in the Holiday Bowl. Holmoe was a big contributor in the bowl victory, picking off a pass in the third quarter and returning it for a touchdown. He also scored a touchdown on a blocked punt against Long Beach State and would finish the year with three interceptions, 61 tackles and was named second-team All-WAC.

Off the field, Holmoe also excelled in the classroom and was enjoying his experience at BYU. In spite of the warnings he had received about attending the LDS-sponsored school as a Lutheran, Holmoe felt comfortable in the environment. "I had great LDS friends and great non-LDS friends and I felt comfortable on both sides," Holmoe said. "I was a member of another faith, an active member, and I went to that church all the way through."

One of Holmoe's LDS friends was Lori Wright, a BYU cheerleader. Lori would later tell the Deseret News, "My mom sent me to BYU to meet a nice Mormon boy, and I came home with the only Lutheran in the whole school." Holmoe began to learn more about the LDS Church through conversations with his new girlfriend. "Lori...taught me a little bit more about the Church. I started going to church with her. I had never gone to church until she asked me to go." The relationship progressed and Holmoe and Wright soon began making wedding plans. "We fell in love and I took the series of discussions but got married outside the Church," he explained. "That was the summer before my senior year, so I went to church my whole senior year."

In his final year on the gridiron for the Cougars, Holmoe was named first-team All-WAC, honorable mention All-American and was selected to play in the Hula Bowl. NFL scouts and teams

Tom Holmoe with Bill Walsh (center)   Photo Focus On Sport/Getty

were well aware of the outstanding defensive back, including San Francisco 49ers head coach and general manager Bill Walsh, who selected Holmoe in the fourth round of the 1983 NFL draft. Backing up Hall of Famer Ronnie Lott for most of his career, Holmoe played seven seasons for the 49ers, winning Super Bowl rings in 1984, 1988 and 1989.

Holmoe had started attending church meetings during his senior season and that continued after he left BYU and joined the 49ers, but he was not ready to become a member of the Church. "I went to church for six years before I was baptized," Holmoe recalled. He had been contemplating baptism for many years, but was hoping for his family's approval, and he wanted to be certain that it was the right decision before making the commitment.

"I was scared," Holmoe said. "I probably wanted to get baptized a long time before I did, but I was scared. I was very scared. It was hard. I was a member of another faith and my family at home was very strong against me joining the Church. Through my great spiritual experiences, going to church, listening and learning about the gospel, not the mistruths, but the truths of the gospel and feeling the Spirit, I was blessed. As I became obedient to some of the principles of the gospel, line upon line, I grew closer and closer. I wanted [my family's approval] but it wasn't going to come. I finally realized that this was my individual choice, no one else's. This was personal. I had a strong testimony, even at the time. It's gotten stronger, but I knew that it was right. I finally decided this is my choice and I'm going to make it."

The testimony and decision was many years in the making, and it didn't come easily. "I had wrestled," Holmoe explained. "You read in the scriptures about wrestling with God. I wrestled long and hard. I was stubborn and prideful, so it didn't help. I knew it. That's why I had to wrestle, because I knew. I was just

Holmoe with 49ers teammate Ronnie Lott and DB coach Ray Rhodes
Photo Michael Zagaris/Getty

hiding."

The bishop of the ward that Tom and Lori attended in the Bay Area played an important role in the process. "I had a really good, young bishop named Jordan Clements, and we were good friends back in California," Holmoe said. "I had numerous home teachers during my six years before my baptism and they would think…they were going to be the ones to baptize me. I let them come in but I really put up a blockade emotionally and spiritually. Then I got a call one day from my bishop and he said, 'Hey Tom, can you come down to my office?' It was the offseason and he said, 'You know I'm your bishop. I hold keys and I'm accountable for your spiritual progress, and because of that I have promptings about the members of our ward, and you're one of my guys.'"

Bishop Clements then asked him, "Have you ever fasted before?" Holmoe replied that he hadn't, and Clements then challenged him: "I want to ask that you and I fast that you receive the answer that I think you are ready to receive. Can you do that?" Holmoe agreed to join the bishop in fasting, unsure of what to expect. "No one had ever asked me to fast," Holmoe explained. "I had prayed a lot. I had prayed and prayed and prayed and I never really seemed to get an answer but it was because every time I prayed, I didn't pray with faith. I'd pray and then I wouldn't do the things necessary to get the message, the answer.

"So I fasted with him and it was a good thing, but I didn't get the answer. So about two weeks passed, and…I was up [in Utah] on vacation. I didn't give up. I just kept praying and praying. I was up here on campus and that's when it happened. It was a very clear impression. It wasn't a vision, it wasn't a voice. I'm not cynical about that, I know that people have seen and heard all that. I don't know how else to describe it but I knew that was the time and it was clear as a bell. It was a strong impression: 'It's time to get baptized - right now.'"

After six years of attending church and many years of praying and pondering, Holmoe knew it was time to act and he didn't delay. "There was a dear friend of mine that was a faculty member on the BYU campus named Joe Wood," Holmoe recalled. "He taught religion and history. He was an older gentleman and he had retired. He was a dear friend, someone I could talk to about the Church. He was a big sports fan and a humble, Christ-centered man. I took every class I could that he taught. I called him out of the blue and said I think I want to get baptized."

"Oh, I knew this day would come," Brother Wood replied upon hearing the news. Unsure of what the next step should be, Holmoe asked Wood, "What do I do?" Wood told him to go and see former BYU equipment manager Floyd Johnson and he would take care of everything.

"I went down to Floyd and said I want to be baptized and he gave me a big hug," Holmoe said. "He said, 'Okay, go see these guys up on campus.' I went to a classroom and the missionaries had an office and I said I need to get baptized on Saturday. They said, 'No, no, you've got to go have the discussions.' I said no, I've already had them, three or four times." The elders were unsure what to make of Tom's request and were not ready to schedule a baptism for a person they had met only a few minutes earlier. A phone call from Johnson helped to clarify the situation and the missionaries were soon on board. Holmoe completed his baptismal interview and the service was scheduled for that Saturday.

Holmoe and his wife were staying with her parents while visiting Provo, so he quickly headed over to their house to share the news. "I went to my in-laws' house and I said, 'Lori, I want to get baptized Saturday.' A few days later, I got baptized on campus in a font in a classroom in the Jesse Knight building."

Holmoe was baptized a member of the Church on February 13, 1988. His father-in-law, Joseph Wright, performed the baptism, and Wood was among Holmoe's close friends who were in attendance.

When Holmoe returned to the 49ers for the 1988 football season, he was comfortable with the decision he had made. "I knew it was the right thing from the time I did it. I went back to the 49ers and the guys on my team were great about it. The non-LDS guys thought I was Mormon anyway because I went to BYU, and hung around Steve Young, Todd Shell, Bart Oates and those guys, the LDS guys that were on the team." Young, Shell and Oates had played with Holmoe at BYU before the four former Cougars were reunited with the 49ers, and they were excited to hear the news.

Adjusting to the LDS way of life is often a struggle for new converts to the Church, but that was not a problem for Holmoe. "I kind of lived my life that way [before baptism]," he explained. "There came a point in time where I lived the Word of Wisdom, paid tithing, those things that people told me for every commandment you're obedient to you receive blessings. I wanted it to be real so I tried it. I wanted it to be true. I wanted to have that confirmation, so when I did that, I think I came along."

A knee injury brought Holmoe's NFL career to an early end after the 1989 season, so he decided to move to the coaching ranks. Both Edwards and Walsh had recognized Holmoe's natural abilities as a coach, and once he expressed an interest in coaching, opportunities quickly followed. After beginning his coaching career as a BYU graduate assistant under Coach Edwards in 1990, Holmoe accepted an offer from Walsh to be the secondary coach at Stanford in 1992. He then returned to the 49ers as the secondary coach in 1994, earning his fourth Super Bowl ring while coaching a defensive backfield that included perennial Pro

Bowlers Deion Sanders, Eric Davis and Merton Hanks.

Holmoe returned to the collegiate coaching ranks in 1996 as the defensive coordinator for the Cal Bears before taking over as the team's head coach from 1997 - 2001. Holmoe had earned his master's degree in athletic administration while coaching with the 49ers and he always had an interest in becoming an athletic director. After finishing his stint at Cal, Holmoe decided to pursue his goals in athletic administration. In 2001, Holmoe and his wife and four children moved to Provo after he accepted a position as the Associate Athletic Director for Development at BYU. After excelling in that position, Holmoe was named the BYU athletic director in March of 2005, a position he never imagined he would one day hold when he first visited BYU as a football recruit nearly 30 years earlier. "If you would have seen me as a freshman at BYU, I don't think very many people would have said that's how that's going to end up," Holmoe said with a laugh.

Looking back, Holmoe recognizes that many people were placed in his life to help him along the path which ultimately led him to where he is today. Dr. Pratley, the emergency room physician who informed Holmoe that his high school football career was over after the broken finger, later became the team doctor at BYU and is one of Holmoe's dear friends to this day. Pratley is just one of many LDS friends, teammates, coaches or professors who touched Holmoe's life over the years.

"There's no question as I look back that there were people in my life and people I met who were placed there," Holmoe said. "There was a young girl that moved into eighth grade at my junior high and her name was Karen Rowley. She was really strong and brave and she was a missionary the first day that she met me. She moved into the school, the new kid on the block, and the first thing she said to me was, 'The water's warm.' I was like,

BYU A.D. Holmoe accepting the Armed Forces Bowl trophy in 2011
Photo Troy Verde/Total Blue Sports

'What?' She said, 'I'm a member of the Mormon Church and I think it's the true church of Christ. The water's warm, that means one day you're going to get baptized.'"

Holmoe wasn't sure what to think of the girl's comment at the time. "I thought, are you kidding me? You don't even know what you're talking about." In spite of the unusual introduction and prediction, the two became close friends. Rowley was one of the first people Holmoe called after he was baptized 15 years later.

In describing his responsibilities as BYU athletic director, Holmoe sees parallels with his Church callings and his experiences as an athlete. "I learned early in sports that you play roles. You don't need to be a star, you just need to play the role to make the team successful. I think that's the same in the Church. There are callings in the Church and every individual has a call in life that your Heavenly Father wants you to do and He wants you to be successful. If you do that call ... then you can grow into other things."

Holmoe's success in athletics and beyond can be attributed to the simple and humble approach he takes in his fulfilling his roles. "I didn't intend to be anything other than good," he said. "I always thought if I did things right and followed the gospel that I'd be on the right track. Good things could happen, tough things could happen, challenges could happen, and I'd just follow that approach. That's all I wanted to do. That's how I am right now [as BYU athletic director]. I'm just in a role. Some roles are bigger than others, but I don't think I'm the top dog. I just have a role."

4

CORBY EASON

It was a difficult and often dangerous life for a child growing up in Columbus, Georgia.   Drug dealers, burglaries and violence were commonplace, and after witnessing it all firsthand, young Corby Eason decided that he didn't want to live that way.

Corby's mother Teresa also wanted a better future for her son. A strict parent, she established a strong religious foundation for her family in the Southern Baptist faith. Teresa was a secretary in the Southern Baptist Church and made sure her son was involved with the religion seven days a week.

Looking back on his childhood, Eason has great love and appreciation for the direction and guidance he received from his mother.

"Being raised by my mom, by herself, that was the best thing that ever happened to me," Eason recalled. "She taught me the key values: my faith, being in tune with our Heavenly Father and Jesus Christ, going to church every Sunday, being part of Bible study every week. That's the only way I made it through my circumstances. I love her so much. Teresa Eason, that's my hero. If it weren't for her and her teaching, I wouldn't be here where I am today."[1]

Life was difficult and money was frequently scarce, but that didn't stop Eason from pursuing his dreams and enjoying his childhood. During summer vacation from school, he and his friends would often pass the time fishing. Unable to afford bait, they would get up early in the morning to collect bait, then jump on their bicycles and ride to the local fishing hole.

Eason was also a gifted athlete and learned to play football in a sandlot near his home. There was no grass field to play on, just the dirt and the rocks, but that didn't deter Eason and his friends. In fact, they played tackle football on that field of dirt and rocks. "I say it made me the athlete I am now, being tough," Eason said. "[I] don't care about pain or anything because I played on these rocks."[2]

Eason excelled at football while at Carver High School, where he was coached by Wallace Davis and Dell McGee. "For his size he was one of the best athletes that a fella ever has the opportunity to work with," Coach Davis recalled. "Off the field, Corby took on the role of a son to me. I was able to interact with him more or less like a father."[3]

After graduating high school, Eason had an opportunity to continue his education and his football career at Erie Community College in Buffalo, New York. He quickly left an impression on the field, recording two interceptions, 15 pass breakups, one forced fumble, five fumble recoveries and a blocked field goal that he returned for a touchdown during his freshman year.

With a reported 4.4 second 40-yard dash, the 5-foot-8-inch cornerback soon received a scholarship offer from Marshall University and was hearing from various schools around the country, including Arizona State, UCLA, Vanderbilt and Maryland. Brigham Young University was not initially one of the schools recruiting Eason, so when a BYU coach came to town to recruit another player, he decided to initiate the conversation on his own.

BYU CB Corby Eason   Photo Troy Verde/Total Blue Sports

"BYU came out to see one of my teammates, Andre Kates," Eason said. "They came to see the other cornerback who played on the other side of me. Coach Higgins came out and was talking to him, but Andre had to come back [to Erie] for one more year. Me, I was eligible out of high school so I could leave without waiting another year.

"My J.C. head coach knew that and didn't want me to talk to Coach Higgins because he knew that I had the opportunity to leave, so he told me to go to class. I disobeyed him, which was wrong, but in the long run it was the right decision for me."

Eason not only disobeyed his coach's orders to go back to class, he also had to hide in the football office until Higgins had finished his meeting with Kates. The meeting took more than two hours, but Eason was determined to wait as long as necessary and remained hidden around a corner until the meeting was over.

"After Coach Higgins talked with Andre in the office, I just stayed outside for around two hours and missed my class," Eason explained. "I got the opportunity to talk to him when he came out and I showed him my highlight tape."

Looking back at that experience, Eason credits his persistence and stubbornness with earning him a chance to play football at Brigham Young University. "By being stubborn and not listening to my coach, that was the difference in me being here at BYU today.

"I have to say, it was the best decision for me in the long run. My coach was a bit upset but I had to do what was best for me and my family, and staying outside that office to talk to a BYU coach was the best decision I made."

Higgins and the rest of the Cougar coaching staff were impressed with the highlight tape and within a week, Eason was on a flight to Utah for an official visit to the Provo campus. Soon after the visit, he officially committed to play for the Cougars and began making plans to move to Provo.

"I really felt comfortable at BYU on my trip and that's why I committed," Eason explained. "It was a clean place and they call it 'Happy Valley,' and I can see why after being there. I couldn't believe how friendly everyone was: the coaching staff, the players, everyone. I just felt at home from the second I arrived on campus."

While Eason was not LDS, he felt very comfortable in BYU's unique environment. When asked after his visit how he felt about BYU's standards and honor code, he replied, "That's a plus in my mind. BYU is a clean place and I really felt comfortable there with everything," Eason said. "I'm going there to play football and get an education. That's what is important and BYU is the place that can best help me focus on those things."

The full-ride scholarship to play football for BYU gave Eason the opportunity to pursue his goals of playing Division I football and earning a college degree. Eason also experienced a spiritual reawakening shortly after beginning his studies in Provo. "Before I came out here I kind of got away from God a little bit, but when I came out here I just got closer and closer to my Heavenly Father," Eason said. "Being here has really helped me grow spiritually and get back to what's really important. It really is a wonderful place and I'm just grateful that I had the chance to be here."

The outgoing Eason soon made friends with his teammates, including fellow defensive backs Brian Logan, Andrew Rich, Brandon Bradley and Scott Johnson. The five teammates spent a lot of time together and Eason was soon singing the praises of BYU when speaking to his family and friends back home in Georgia.

"I talk to my other friends back home about how it is out here," Eason said during his first year at BYU. "I even called my best friend Jarmon Fortson, the starting wide receiver for Florida State, and told him how it is out here. I talked to him about how the people treat us out here. They treat us great.

BYU CBs Brian Logan (7) and Corby Eason (25)

Photo Troy Verde/Total Blue Sports

"It's been great and this has been one of the best places I've ever been," Eason continued. "Actually, I love it here better than I do at home. I mean, the community is so friendly out here. I'm from the South and things are kind of different down there, but out here they don't care and like you as is. It's like family out here."

As non-LDS players who were part of the same recruiting class, Eason and Logan soon became close friends and their discussion topics included their religious beliefs. BYU head coach Bronco Mendenhall took a special interest in assisting Eason, Logan and the other non-LDS players on the team with their spiritual growth. Looking back on that experience, Logan described the unique relationship.

"Coach Mendenhall is a special head coach," Logan said. "I always joke around with Corby that Coach Mendenhall is like this prophet because he has this glow about him. He really is a spiritual person and the thing I liked is he has never, never, ever thrown or pushed his faith on me. I know this goes for the rest of the guys as well. He's always tried to help me out to become stronger in my faith and my personal relationship with God."

Eason echoed his teammate's thoughts, recounting how BYU helped him to get back to the religious ideals his mother had taught him.

"Being here has really helped me grow spiritually. It really is a wonderful place because it's really helped me get back to what's important and grow closer to God." Eason noted at the time how Coach Mendenhall helped him to grown as a Baptist, and how he made sure that those players who were not LDS participated in religious firesides and were able to share their testimonies.

"It's wonderful because Coach Mendenhall wants everyone to be involved in the firesides," said Eason back in 2010. "Those are not just for members of the LDS faith, but for us too. I plan on talking at one of the firesides, as well as Brian Logan. Coach

Mendenhall wants us to share our experiences about how we are disciples of Christ, and that's going to be wonderful. I can't wait to have that experience.

"Looking back as a kid and seeing my mom, being a single mother, taking me to church every Sunday, I remember she would go to Bible study every night and I would go to the nursery and play with the kids. Even when I got in high school she would make me go to church youth groups, so now that I'm in college it's great to have that support from Coach Mendenhall and the rest of the staff here at BYU."

Eason summarized his feelings on Coach Mendenhall and the impact he had on his players, both as football players and as men. "You know, with most coaches it's about the X's and the O's, and not about the game of life," said Eason. "With Coach Mendenhall, his first priority is the game of life and he wants you to become a better father, a better brother and to help you grow as a better human being as well as a football player. I really appreciate that because we're learning the X's and O's of success on and off the field. Football will only last for a couple of years, but being a better father, brother or person will last forever."

Another eye-opening experience for Logan and Eason was their interaction with the Cougar fan base. On September 5, 2009, the BYU Cougars opened their season by taking on the No. 3 Oklahoma Sooners. Eason and Logan were understandably thrilled to be playing in their first Division I game. The fact that this would be the inaugural Cowboys Classic game played in the brand new $1.6 billion Cowboys Stadium before a national TV audience only added to the excitement.

The Cougars launched their season in style, pulling out a thrilling come-from-behind victory over the Sooners. When the team flight arrived back in Provo at about 1:45 in the morning, the Cougar football team was greeted by a throng of cheering fans.

"The fans are great," said Logan when asked about that

experience. "It's just, wow! I love our fans here at BYU and think they are the greatest. It's been an unbelievable experience here and I get goose bumps just talking about it. It has been great and I have no complaints or anything bad to say about anything about this university, the people or the community. I just love it here. I just love it."

Eason was also at a loss for words when talking about the fan support and the overall friendliness of the student body at BYU. "I mean, my first day when I came in and everyone was like, 'How are you doing? How you doing?,' I was shocked. Most of the time people will just stare at the freshmen and don't say anything to them, but everybody is friendly out here like family.

"It's like I've been out here for four years. It's been a great experience out here and all the fans love you and every day when I walk with my BYU gear on people ask me if I'm on the football team. When I tell them yeah they say, 'Thank you and congratulations and I hope you do well.' Everyone is just friendly out here and I love it. I love it out here. I even told my parents to come out here, and they told me as soon as they get some vacation time they're coming."

Eason played in 12 of 13 games as a sophomore as he got his feet wet at the Division I level. As he began his junior season in 2010, Eason became a much greater force on the football field. He became part of the regular rotation, backing up friend and teammate Brandon Bradley at the boundary corner position. Given increased playing time, Eason quickly left his mark.

In addition to 22 tackles, including 20 solo takedowns, Eason also had 3.5 sacks. The sack number was good enough for second-best on the team – an amazing accomplishment for a backup cornerback. Eason also excelled in the classroom, being named to the Mountain West Conference All-Academic team for the second year in a row.

While Eason was raising his performance on the field and

Eason's friends and teammates Andrew Rich (top) and Brandon Bradley (bottom) Photos Troy Verde/Total Blue Sports

continuing to shine in the classroom, he was also experiencing some big changes off the field. With two games remaining in the regular season, Eason announced to his teammates and coaches that he would be baptized a member of the LDS Church.

Looking back on his conversion process, Eason described how every morning he would look out his window, see Mount Timpanogos and thank God he was in Provo. "Just being out here and learning more about the Church has made me happy. I believe the Church is true," Eason said.

When asked how he came to believe that, Eason said, "I found out the Church was true through prayer. I felt the Spirit and felt the Holy Ghost like I haven't before.

"I just remember on my first day in Provo I felt something. I'm a curious guy. I always want to know how things work, why things work. When I came to BYU I did everything that I was supposed to do. I followed the honor code and for some reason I still wasn't as happy as my other teammates.

"I was curious about what I was missing and I started talking to Andrew Rich and Brandon Bradley more about the Church and praying about it and praying more about it and reading the scriptures, the same scriptures that Joseph Smith read, James 1, verse 5. Just reading this scripture and just pondering about my decision, it was a wonderful feeling."[4]

As Eason walked down into the baptismal font on November 18, 2010, he saw many familiar faces standing quietly in support.

The person who had the honor of performing Eason's baptism also happened to be the person he played behind: Bradley. Bradley, who joined the Church along with his family while he was a high school student in Florida, played a special role in Eason's spiritual journey.

"Ever since I've been here, I've been talking to [Bradley] about the experience he went through with his family and the Church," said Eason. "I love it and really understood more about it. He would answer my questions and was always there for me. He was really a big help to me in learning and understanding."

"I'm excited too!" said Bradley a few days before the baptism. "It's been a long road for Corby and I've been able to sit in on some of the discussions, and it's been good just learning and understanding and living by how he's been taught. I'm excited for him and he's really excited about it and looking forward to it. I'll be there to support him every step of the way."

Without reviewing any film, Coach Mendenhall offered Bradley a scholarship while he was still serving a mission in São Paulo, Brazil. Bradley had committed to Louisville out of high school and wasn't sure that BYU was the right place for him, but the decision to attend BYU after his mission came by way of an answered prayer.

While at BYU, Bradley still had one more missionary task to fulfill even though he no longer wore a missionary nametag. "I've tried to do whatever I could to help [Eason] understand the questions he may have," a humble Bradley said with a laugh. "I let him know it's going to be a tough decision, but it's the right decision. I was basically just being me and doing whatever I can and supported him in every step of the way, so I can't take too much credit for it. I think Heavenly Father deserves most of the credit."

Meanwhile, Eason was confirmed by E.J. Caffaro, Director of the Student Athlete Academic Center at BYU. "He's been a great help to me, and so I asked him if he would do it," said Eason. Those in attendance at the baptismal service described Eason as happy, humble and sincere. Three of Corby's teammates sang a song and Coach Mendenhall gave a short talk.

Eason's decision to investigate the LDS faith came by way of the example set forth by his teammates and the happiness he witnessed in their lives. "That really just caught my eye, seeing how happy everyone was out here all the time," Eason said. "No matter what everyone was going through, everyone was just happy. It was just different and everyone has really strong family values, and that was a great example to me."

Head coach Bronco Mendenhall was at a loss for words when asked about his cornerback's decision to enter the waters of baptism. Fumbling to find the right words, Mendenhall reverently looked down towards the ground and did his best to express his feelings.

"It's just one of the bright spots of my coaching career here," Coach Mendenhall said. "I love Corby and he's just a fantastic kid, and I love him, and just really I'm proud of him for his decision. I don't know what else to say."

As Eason walked off the practice field two days prior to his baptism in a hurry to attend a class, he seemed at peace. The smile he always wore when walking off the practice field seemed a little wider, his face a little brighter. "I'm just excited and really happy about my decision," Eason said. "The Church is true."

As Eason completed his junior season, he had more exciting experiences ahead of him. In January of 2011, he married his sweetheart Rebecca. When spring practice began a couple months later, Eason was slotted as the starter at field corner and found himself one of the leaders on the Cougar defense.

After a rough start with some disappointing losses, the Cougars finished the 2011 season 10-3, capped off by a win over Tulsa in the Armed Forces Bowl. Eason finished the year with 46 tackles, seventh-best on the team and tops among the cornerbacks. He also finished the year with 14 pass breakups, which tied with teammate Preston Hadley for ninth best in the nation. Eason's accomplishments on the field were recognized by the national media, as he was named to both the Phil Steele All-Independent First Team and the FBS All-Independent Team.

In January 2012, just one month after his final game in a Cougar uniform, Eason was sealed to his wife Rebecca in the Las

Photo Troy Verde/Total Blue Sports

Vegas LDS temple. Three months later, he earned his bachelor's degree in psychology, receiving academic honors from the NCAA with a 3.4 grade point average.

Eason discussed his time at BYU with Dick Harmon of the Deseret News in July of 2012. "I remember when I first came to college, we were playing San Diego State and the team drove by the San Diego Temple. I said to myself one day I wanted to go inside that building. This past year, on our honeymoon, Rebecca and I did go in that temple. It was wonderful and I feel so blessed. My relatives back home, the younger kids look up to me for going to college and trying to make something out of myself.

"I feel fortunate that I got go to play major college football, get an education, meet my wife and have the life I do. I'm a lucky man and coming to Provo changed my life. Many of my friends I grew up with that I talk to — they are happy for me and what is happening."[5]

Eason's accomplishments both on the field and off have not gone unnoticed by his family, friends, coaches and teammates. Carver High School coach Wallace Davis said, "That is the greatest feeling to know that a young man who almost had his hands tied from the start overcame some hurdles that the average person couldn't overcome. And to get where he is at this point is very, very extraordinary."[6]

Eason described the great happiness he has found since coming to BYU and finding the LDS Church. "My family has seen how I've grown as a man. There's some athletes that come here wanting too much to be different, but the more you want to be different and the more you try to be different, the worse your experience will be. I know that for myself. But if you just do what is right, then you're going to be happy. The happiness I've found being at BYU and being a member of the Church — I can't even explain to you how much more happy I am as a person."[7]

Coach Mendenhall is also inspired by what Eason has

accomplished and will accomplish in the future. "He's really fit in well here," Mendenhall said. "He's become a member of the Church, he's become a team leader — a team favorite. He's married now, and when he goes back home he'll be a great example to those in his neighborhood. It's a pretty inspiring story. It just shows that when a young man wants this experience, no matter where he's from, no matter what race or what faith, that it can be a great experience."[8]

5

TY DETMER

The last place one would expect to find former BYU-great Ty Detmer is on the campus of the University of Utah, yet that's where he agreed to meet during the summer of 2012 and talk about his BYU experience. Cougar fans need not worry about him changing his allegiances, though, as he was only there to take his daughter to a camp for high school soccer players.

Detmer was born in San Marcos, Texas, located between Austin and San Antonio. His father, Sonny, was a high school football coach for many years, and he coached other sports too, although football was his passion.

Because of his father, Detmer grew up around the local football team. He also grew up playing sports, and said he always had a ball, bat, or other piece of athletic equipment in his hands.

While attending Southwest High School in San Antonio, he competed in football, basketball, baseball, track and even golf. If nothing else, golf would allow him to get out of class on occasion, he noted.

Despite all-district honors in basketball and all-state honors in baseball, football was Detmer's first love. It was what he looked forward to, and what he enjoyed the most. It was also what he was best at, having eventually been named the Texas Player of the Year as a senior quarterback.

Soon, the Texas gunslinger sought to take his prowess to the college level.

"At that time there weren't many teams throwing the ball, and we threw it quite a bit in high school and ran a pro-style offense," Detmer said, "so I was looking for that similar situation to go into, and [my] goal was to ... play in the NFL at some point. So as you're looking at schools, for me, I needed to find something that fit my personality and skill set. I wasn't the biggest, fastest guy, but was smart, knew the game and could throw it."

Detmer wasn't highly recruited, as BYU ended up being his only offer. He had seen BYU win the 1984 national championship, three years before he was to enter college. He said it opened his eyes to there being a team out there that was doing what his high school was doing – throwing the ball around. He also had a lot of respect for the Cougar program and what it had done with past quarterbacks.

So, he drove out to Utah – his first-ever visit to the state – the summer before his senior year and met head coach LaVell Edwards. Coming from Texas, he enjoyed being around mountains for the first time, and was also struck by the fresh, cool air compared to the humidity back home. He also noticed how clean and pristine the campus was.

Coach Edwards has joked in the past about his first meeting with Detmer, saying that he was expecting someone like John Elway to walk into his office, but instead got Pee-wee Herman. Detmer didn't look the part of a high school All-American, and without internet recruiting services like Scout and Rivals or online highlight videos in those days, the coaches didn't fully know what to expect of Detmer.

"Nowadays, shoot, the way recruiting is with Rivals and all that, I don't know if I'd have gotten recruited out of high school just 'cause of the size, and they're looking for guys that are 6'3" and 200 pounds, and I was 6-foot, 165 pounds coming into his office," Detmer said.

Edwards "was probably wondering what he was getting into," Detmer said with a laugh.

Nevertheless, his underwhelming stature aside, Detmer accepted his BYU offer. He had no real interest in other schools, nor did he take any other recruiting trips.

After his commitment that summer before his senior year, however, there were some big-name schools that expressed interest. Michigan contacted him, and so did Miami, which was ironic given how Detmer would cross paths with the Hurricanes down the road. But Detmer held strong to his commitment to BYU.

And yet, even though he was going to BYU, Detmer had little understanding of the Church of Jesus Christ of Latter-day Saints.

"Really didn't have much knowledge at all of it," he said. "As far as I knew, I didn't know any members. Just didn't know much about the Church at all."

But, his parents did ingrain Christian values in him while growing up, and Heavenly Father and Jesus Christ were talked about in his home.

"I grew up Methodist but we didn't go to church a lot," said Detmer. "In high school I joined the Fellowship of Christian Athletes and started going to church a little bit more on my own and becoming, I guess, more religious at that point."

Being in a wholesome environment appealed to Detmer.

"One of the reasons I wanted to go to BYU was my high school was kind of a rough area, and I was kind of the designated driver from early on. My buddies would party every weekend, and I'd make sure nobody got in trouble, and I didn't drink but I was there kind of making sure everybody got home alright."

He said he grew tired of that atmosphere and looked forward

BYU QB Ty Detmer   Photo Mike Powell/Getty

to being at BYU where he wouldn't have to babysit everybody. Despite his limited understanding of the LDS faith, he appreciated its standards and values.

Of course, he also came to BYU to sling the pigskin around. At BYU he saw past quarterbacks' awards and All-American pictures displayed all around, and said he hoped someday he'd have something of his own displayed for others to see. He added that he had a lot of admiration and respect for the players that came before, and really appreciated the opportunity to fill their shoes.

After redshirting his first year at BYU in 1987, Detmer got his first opportunity to play in the 1988 season opener against Wyoming when starting quarterback Sean Covey got a concussion. He started off well, throwing a touchdown on his first series.

"Okay, this is just like high school, nothing different," he thought.

However, his next five series featured four interceptions and a fumble, and BYU lost 24-14.

"It was a real learning experience for me that it's not just gonna happen; I really gotta buckle down and work harder in practice and tune in more," Detmer said.

As a backup, he learned that he had to be ready and work hard in practice as though he could play at any time. He did indeed play a good amount as a redshirt freshman, and came off the bench in the Freedom Bowl to lead BYU to a 20-17 victory over Colorado, which he felt established him as the starter for the next season.

Meanwhile, he credited assistant coaches such as Norm Chow, Roger French and Lance Reynolds with helping him develop.

"They taught you the game and allowed you to kind of be an individual and play, and as I earned it I think I had a lot of freedom within the offense to audible, change plays or call my own sometimes, and I really appreciate that from them."

Detmer put up some big numbers as a sophomore, including what was a new bowl record at the time with 594 yards of total offense against Penn State in the Holiday Bowl. What Cougar fans remember most from that year, however, was his performance against the rival Utah Utes.

The previous season, the Utes had laid it on the Cougars up in Salt Lake City. They won 57-28 in a game in which Detmer played most of the second half. Utah quarterback Scott Mitchell, as Detmer put it, tore the Cougars up. So, BYU was looking to redeem itself the following year.

"We were looking forward to that game," said Detmer. "We heard the talk for a whole year and couldn't wait for the game that year."

The Cougs jumped out to a 49-0 lead in the second quarter after scoring touchdowns on all seven of their first drives. When the smoke had cleared, BYU won 70-31.

Mitchell actually got injured in practice the week of the rivalry game and thus didn't get to play, which Detmer said probably took some of the wind out of Utah's sails. But given BYU's offensive efficiency, it surely wouldn't have mattered.

"I always felt like he owed me about 200 more yards, 'cause had he been playing, I still would have been in the game probably a little bit," said Detmer, who barely played in the second half.

Detmer really got to show the country what he could do when BYU hosted No. 1 Miami the following year in a nationally televised showdown. BYU has already played one game, but it was the season opener for the defending national champion Hurricanes, who had won three national titles in the 1980s.

The controversial Hurricanes, with their thuggish reputation, were a stark contrast from the clean-cut Cougars. The Miami program and its players were known for their brashness and off-the-field scandals. Detmer said they were a pretty cocky bunch, and he and his teammates were excited for the opportunity to play them.

BYU had played at Miami two years before, a game in which Detmer got some playing time. He threw three interceptions – one for a touchdown – but said it was a good learning experience, and that it prepared him to face the Hurricanes and their speed in his junior year.

The Cougars had turnover issues again in the rematch – four fumbles and an interception – but kept fighting. Detmer said the mindset early on was to try and neutralize their pass rush and slow them down with quick, short completions. BYU went into halftime with a 17-14 lead against the top-ranked team in the country.

"We kind of hung in there, and built a lead at halftime I think, and gained a lot of confidence as we went along that we could do this."

Detmer had to hang in there physically as well after taking a shot to the chin that required stitches at halftime.

"The guy caught me just as I was releasing the ball. It was complete for about 25 yards over to Chris Smith, so it was worth the hit," he said with a laugh.

If there's a play from that game that sticks out to Detmer, it would be the go-ahead touchdown in the third quarter, as that is the highlight that's been shown the most over the years.

With BYU trailing 21-20, the offense reached the red zone. Detmer dropped back to pass, and with no one open initially, he moved around in the pocket. Two Hurricane defenders converged on him from opposite directions, but he stepped out of the way at the last moment, sending the two colliding foolishly into each other. Detmer then found his man for the score. After a two-point conversion, the Cougars led 28-21, which would end up being the final score.

With 406 passing yards and three touchdowns, Detmer had helped topple the top team in the country, and fans began pouring

USC Trojans QB Todd Marinovich (#13), BYU Cougars QB Ty Detmer (#14), ASU Sun Devils QB Paul Justin (#10)

Photo Bernstein Associates/Getty

out onto the field by the thousands. As this was new to Detmer, he didn't quite know what to do.

"My first initial reaction was, 'Man, I'm gonna be the last one in the locker room. Coach Edwards is gonna be giving the post-game talk and I'm gonna walk in the middle of it and it's gonna be awkward.'"

So, he fought his way through the swarm of fans and went into the locker room, only to find that he was the only person in there. With no one to celebrate with, he waited alone for about five minutes.

Looking back, Detmer acknowledged that "I probably could have gotten away with being the last one in. [Coach Edwards] probably wouldn't have been mad."

Thanks to that Miami game and his other performances, Detmer found himself a candidate for the Heisman, an award given to the nation's best college football player. It's the most prestigious individual player award in college football – if not all of sports.

The school went out of its way to promote him, distributing tie-shaped pamphlets adorned with the phrase "Five good reasons the Heisman race should end in a Ty." On the inside were five quotes, given by Coach Edwards as well as players and coaches from other teams, praising Detmer.

"I thought it was pretty neat at the time," he said about BYU promoting him. "It's one of those things you kind of put up with a little bit too. But I think [playing for] a school like BYU where you're trying to get on the map and they're trying to do everything they can to get you out there was pretty neat, and so at that time you're just going along with it and hoping to do good and make sure it's [not] all for naught."

A number of past BYU quarterbacks had been Heisman candidates, and in five different years a Cougar even finished in the top three for Heisman voting, but none of them had won the elusive and prestigious award.

That all changed in 1990 when Detmer won it, something he wasn't expecting.

"I think that's one of the biggest surprises there is," he said. "Nobody knows, and there's rarely any information leaked about the Heisman and who's really gonna win it until they open that envelope, so it was a pretty neat experience."

For Detmer, winning the Heisman wasn't just a great achievement personally, but also one for Coach Edwards and the BYU program, which had waited so long to get over the hump.

A few months after winning the Heisman, another major event took place in Detmer's life when he was baptized. He had been influenced over the years by his coaches, teammates and others at BYU.

Among those that impacted Detmer was running back Eric Mortensen, who was also his roommate. They lived in a house along with some others, and Mortensen was the only one that was a member of the Church.

"It was three-on-one sometimes, three of us nonmembers against him as the only member, and we had many discussions and he always just held strong to his testimony," said Detmer. "And I always respected that of him, and his conviction. And he chose not to go on a mission to pursue football but he was a missionary to me, lived the gospel, and was just a great example for me."

Detmer was also motivated by his girlfriend at BYU. They had been friends for a long time, and when they started dating, Detmer knew it was serious. So, he said he knew he needed to really dig in deep and learn more about the Church.

So, he took the missionary discussions in the home of BYU's head trainer George Curtis, and found that the principles of the restored gospel were in line with what he had grown up believing and how he believed one should live their life. He described it as a simple conversion.

Detmer's parents were initially concerned with the path he was taking, especially after being shown anti-Mormon material back in Texas, but he was able to alleviate their concerns.

"I had a chance to go home, talk to them about it and just let them know that nothing's changed," he said. "My beliefs are a little different, but I still believe in Christ."

His parents accepted his new faith, and years down the road after Detmer had a family, they attended the baptism for each of his children.

The football offices at BYU received some mail for Detmer from complete strangers criticizing his decision to join the Church, but Detmer just laughs about that now. He said he believes BYU football secretary Shirley Johnson shielded him from some of the hate mail.

Back in Utah, Detmer found acceptance instead of resistance. He was baptized the same night as his teammate Peter Tuipulotu, and along the way, some of his other teammates embraced the gospel as well.

"You'd see guys, and every year there'd be a handful or a couple that would join the Church," said Detmer. "To me it was they were making a life decision, and [I] never really thought much about it. So it was just part of going to school here, to see people take on new responsibilities or dedicate themselves more to religion than maybe they'd grown up with."

After marrying his girlfriend that summer, Detmer then entered his senior season. It got off to a bad start, however, with BYU losing its first three games.

"We had a different team. We'd lost quite a few guys from the year before and had a young group, and so we started out with a tough schedule: Florida State in the Pigskin Classic in Anaheim, and then at Penn State, at UCLA, and that team probably wasn't quite ready for those types of games on the road. So there was

Detmer with the Philadelphia Eagles in 1996

Photo Rick Stewart/Getty

some frustrating times, but then we just continued to improve and by the end of the year we were a good football team. [I] take a lot of pride in hanging in there and being a leader on that team and helping that group kind of get to where we finished up."

After those first three games, the Cougs wouldn't lose again. However, they did have two tie games, as this was before college football allowed overtime.

One of those ties was an exciting comeback for BYU – Detmer referred to these as 'typical BYU type of games' – against San Diego State.

Trailing SDSU 45-17 in the second half with the WAC title on the line, all hope seemed lost. Yet, Detmer and company did not throw in the towel.

"I think we got in [our] two-minute offense and just said 'Let's go see what happens.' And our defense stepped up, got the ball back, and it's just one of those things where things started clicking and we just got rolling on fire, and they got a little conservative with the lead trying to run some clock so we couldn't get the ball back. And the defense would stop them, and next thing you know we're in the end zone again."

The Cougars stormed back and ended up with a final score of 52-52, thanks to Detmer's 599 passing yards and six touchdowns. A tie was enough to send BYU to the Holiday Bowl.

Detmer finished his BYU career with a whopping 59 NCAA records, and he also tied for three others. He's not sure how many of them still stand today, though the ones that stood out in his mind have been broken: career touchdowns, career yardage and single-season yardage.

"It was fun having people break them because then you get interviewed and you get to go back and relive some of those moments, so it was fun."

His career stats would be even more impressive if his bowl game stats were included, but the NCAA didn't start officially counting bowl stats until years later. Detmer said he doesn't think it would make much of a difference though.

Given his prolific career, Detmer was admitted to the College Football Hall of Fame in 2012.

"It was pretty neat. Got calls from a lot of teammates, coaches, people I knew, and it's fun to go back and relive old times and talk about it and some of those things. You're always appreciative of things like that, that people appreciated the work you put in and the things you did."

Following 14 years in the NFL – mostly as a backup – Detmer left the game for five years. During this time he was asked by people whether he was ever going to coach, and while his response was never say never, he was enjoying the free time he had.

Some family friends, who had a son attending St. Andrew's Episcopal School in Austin, asked Detmer if the school's athletic director could call him and inquire about coaching the football team. He agreed to it, and as he talked about coaching he became excited about the opportunity.

So, in 2010 he joined the coaching ranks and took over a struggling program. With just 38 players at the time, 18 of which were freshmen, the team went 0-10. The team went 3-7 the following season, and he entered his third season as head coach with a roster of about 60 players. By his fourth year, he hopes to have an ideal composition of seniors and juniors.

"You find you can't beat age and maturity and experience," said Detmer.

With that added experience, he anticipates the program will continue to grow.

"We're getting better. We still have some work to do and there are challenges, but all the kids are excited about football and more kids are playing, and [there's] just more excitement about it."

As a first-time coach, he has been influenced by his coaches over the years, including Edwards and the others he had at BYU.

"I'm not a real drill sergeant type of coach. My dad's not that way either. But you want the kids there to learn the game, so I'm more of a teacher. [I] want them to learn why we're doing things, learn the game, and that's the way it was at BYU for me. Same type of thing. Every now and then you got to get fired up and crack the whip, but I think when they see that side they know I'm serious and we gotta get going, but overall I want them to enjoy it, have fun. It's a short period of time in their life, as it was for me with high school. College goes quick. So, enjoy the time you're out there, work hard, be the best you can, but enjoy it at the same time."

When it comes to coaching, many wonder when Detmer will return to Provo. Regarding how often people ask him about coaching at BYU, he said with a laugh, "All the time. Never been offered a job. There's a lot of rumors floating around. And again, my answer is never say never, but I enjoy the high school lifestyle where you have some time off to take your daughter to camp and do the other things during the offseason [since] you're not on the road recruiting and things like that. Right now I really enjoy what I'm doing, where I'm doing it. You take it a year at a time. At some point they'll probably get tired of me there, and then [I'll] explore other options."

Rumors were particularly rampant after the 2010 season when the Cougar staff was being shaken up. Quarterback coach Brandon Doman was expected to become offensive coordinator, and Detmer was said to be a top candidate to take over coaching the quarterbacks. Instead, Doman continued coaching the quarterbacks despite becoming offensive coordinator.

"There's no opening or anything," said Detmer with a smile. "There never was. I could have, I guess, maybe coached kickers or something, but it wouldn't have been too successful."

Detmer at halftime of the BYU vs. Univ. of Washington game in 2010

Photo Troy Verde/Total Blue Sports

Months after the shakeup on the staff, Doman called up Detmer to touch base, address the rumors, and gauge his interest in possibly returning to BYU sometime down the road, but fans will have to continue to wait for the time being.

As for his personal life, Detmer is now the father of four daughters between the ages of 11 and 19. Not having any sons may seem difficult for someone with such a passion for sports and the outdoors, but Detmer doesn't think he's missing anything by having only girls.

"They all like to get out and get dirty, play around, and they're athletic and enjoy the outdoors, so I wouldn't know what to do with a boy. I don't think it would be too much different."

He does of course get to work with plenty of young men through coaching, and has also done so through numerous church callings, including serving in his stake's young men's presidency.

"That's always fun for me," he said. "Now, they're young enough that they don't remember who I was, or their parents have to tell them about me, which is good. They just think I'm one of the guys out there hauling them around or helping out, and so I think it's fun for them to hear some of the stories and figure out who I was and some of that as well. Hopefully I'm setting the right example for them and helping them with any of their problems or issues that are going on in their life. There's a lot going on today for kids."

Over the years, having the gospel in his life has helped give him perspective, particularly to see that losing a football game wasn't going to matter down the road.

"Obviously you want to play good and take pride in what you're putting out on the field, but at the end of the day it's your relationship with your family and Heavenly Father, and those are the most important things out there. And so I think raising kids, and having those values to be able to instill in them, definitely has made a difference in my life and it's helped me through some tough times, through the good times, all those things, to maintain a balanced life and know what's really important at the end of the day."

Detmer hopes that through his football accomplishments at BYU, he was able to bring some positive attention to the Church of Jesus Christ of Latter-day Saints.

"I guess people see BYU and maybe ask a few more questions about the school and the Church and tie the two together, and so I think me being out there representing BYU and now the Church hopefully has been a positive for the school and the Church as well."

He usually visits Utah at least once a year, and also keeps in touch with various teammates. All in all, Detmer looks back fondly on his time at BYU and the people there, from his teammates and coaches to all the fans.

"It was the perfect place for me to go to school, just with the lifestyle like I said I was looking for, and being up in the mountains with the outdoors part of it was a big piece for me too. It was the perfect fit for me, so couldn't ask for [more] things. I'd take a few throws back maybe, a couple reads, but other than that I couldn't ask for a better place to go to school. I think that time of your life you're becoming an adult, you're on your own, you're figuring out your own set of values and how you want to live your life. And for me it was a great place to go and do that and be able to create that foundation that built on that foundation that my parents had set and go from there."

6

SETE AULAI

Originally from the small village of Vailoa on the island of Savai'i, Samoa, Sete Aulai grew up in a Christian home in Carson, California. Located on the southwest border of Compton in Los Angeles County, Carson had its share of problems with gangs, drugs and violence. Growing up in the area shaped Aulai, and like the streets of Carson, he became tough. That toughness, along with exceptional physical strength, made Aulai a natural football player.

By the time he reached high school, Aulai was performing well on the football field and in the classroom, garnering numerous accolades in the process. Coaches from the top football programs on the West Coast were soon aware of the young offensive lineman. The recruiting attention increased as Aulai approached his senior season.

"I went to Carson High and I started two years on varsity," Aulai recalled. "In my junior year I made second-team All-Area and first-team All-Marine League. I got invited to the USC camp, the UCLA camp and the Nike camp. My senior year I made first-team All-Area, first-team All-League and I made the All-Regional Team. I made Scholar Athlete with a 3.1 [GPA] and the National

Honor Roll. I'm not the smartest kid in the world, but I try."

However, despite his success in the classroom and on the field, Aulai never received a coveted scholarship offer from the Pac-10 schools that were courting him at the time. "I got letters from everybody but nobody offered," Aulai said. "I got letters from just about everyone from the Pac-10 like SC, UCLA, Oregon, Oregon State, Arizona, Arizona State, Washington and Washington State, but nobody offered."

Undeterred by the lack of a Division I scholarship, Aulai was determined to continue his football career at the next level. Rather than walk on at a Division I school, he opted to go the junior college route, signing with El Camino College in neighboring Torrance, California.

Soon after strapping on the pads for the El Camino Warriors, the big offensive guard began to build an impressive football resume that once again attracted the attention of Division I coaches. "My freshman year at El Camino, I played all 11 games and made Honorable Mention All-Conference," said Aulai. "It's the toughest conference in the U.S. Trust me. Going into my sophomore year I was voted Preseason All-American. At the end of the season I made first-team All-Mission Conference, first-team All-State, second-team All-American." Aulai also received El Camino's Helmet Award, given to the team's top offensive lineman each season. While he started at guard for El Camino, Aulai also played some fullback, a testament to his exceptionally quick feet. He capped off his numerous awards by being named a Junior College Athletic Bureau first-team All-American.

As the scholarship offers began to roll in during his sophomore season at El Camino, Aulai knew he had an important choice to make. Brigham Young University was one of many schools that had offered him a scholarship, but he didn't know a lot about the BYU football program or the LDS Church which sponsored the school. He decided to learn more and scheduled an official

BYU center Sete Aulai   Photo Troy Verde/Total Blue Sports

recruiting visit in late January of 2005 to see things at BYU firsthand.

The visit to Provo went far better than he ever expected. "I tripped out here to visit this past weekend and I just loved it," Aulai said in an interview with Total Blue Sports the weekend after his visit. "It was nothing like I imagined. I loved it up there! It was like nothing else and nothing like from where I'm from."

When asked what it was about Provo and the BYU campus that had made such an impression, he said, "I liked the facilities over there and everything was topnotch and state of the art. I want to be in a clean environment and that's where I like to be at and not a dirty place."

Aulai was so impressed by his visit that he placed a phone call to Coach Bronco Mendenhall the day after his official visit. "I verbally committed," Aulai said. "I did that on Sunday to Coach Mendenhall. My parents support me 100 percent and they're happy. I chose BYU because I like the clean campus and environment. I got to know the players and the coaches really well. I like the coaches and the players."

As a Samoan, Aulai was also excited by the number of Polynesian players on the BYU roster. "Another reason why I chose BYU is because I like to be around Polys," Aulai explained. "I just feel comfortable being around people like me."

Aulai was excited to begin his career at BYU, but there was one remaining hurdle that he still had to overcome: cutting his hair to comply with the BYU honor code. "The only bad thing I didn't like is I had to cut my hair and it was almost to the middle of my back," Aulai said. "It was down past my shoulders. That was the only bad thing, but other than that it's all good." Within two days of his on-campus visit and commitment to sign with the Cougars, Aulai sheared his Samoan locks and was anxiously preparing for his move to Provo. "Oh, you don't know how much I'm excited," he said. "I want to come back to BYU already. I want to play."

When Aulai arrived at BYU prior to the 2005 season, the football program was struggling. Bronco Mendenhall had recently taken over as head coach and the Cougars were looking to bounce back from a string of losing seasons. Aulai figured to be a part of that turnaround. After redshirting in 2005, he moved from his junior college position of guard and became the starting center for the Cougars in 2006.

Aulai was known for working especially hard in the weight room and he soon became one of the strongest players on the BYU football team. Fellow offensive lineman Travis Bright, nicknamed "The Hulk" after breaking numerous weight room records at BYU, was one of Aulai's lifting partners, along with Jake Kuresa and Eddie Keele. Aulai credited his teammates for helping him achieve success in the weight room.

"Jake is my big uso [Samoan for brother]," said Aulai. "I look up to him and I watch everything he does. My lifting group was me, Jake, Travis and Eddie, and ever since I've been lifting with those guys, I've gotten stronger. Because of those three guys, I've gotten a lot stronger. Lifting with the three strongest guys on the team has really helped me out a lot. Now I'm right behind them. I'm number four—the fourth strongest on the team because I've been lifting with those guys."

Aulai was very popular among his teammates, and during spring camp of 2006 they dubbed him with a fitting nickname. Sitting on a bench just outside the locker room doors after a full contact scrimmage, Aulai was catching his breath when his nickname was born.

"That's The Rhinoceros right there," said defensive end Kyle Luekenga while pointing to Aulai. "Sete 'The Rhinoceros' is probably the quickest offensive lineman we have. He has quick feet like a d-lineman. I think he did a lot of jump roping when he was growing up."

Of the three species of rhinoceros, the largest stands six feet

Aulai and Travis Bright (74) blocking against Wyoming

Photo Troy Verde/Total Blue Sports

tall and will defend its territory with reckless tenacity. The rhinoceros is not the tallest of the mammals roaming the Asian and African plains, but it is exceptionally quick for its size and will battle predators with a fierce charge. The rhinoceros nickname seemed a perfect fit for the 6-foot, 313-pound Aulai, who possessed an on-field mean streak of his own.

Aulai gained additional notoriety when he arrived for the first day of fall camp in August of 2006 with a full beard, sporting what was famously described as the "Samoan lumberjack look." Inquiring media members immediately asked him about the facial hair, a rare sight at Brigham Young University. Aulai explained that he had been diagnosed with razor bumps, allowing him to receive one of the ever-elusive BYU beard cards. The long hair from his junior college days was long gone, but Aulai was allowed to play out his BYU career with a beard.

The nickname and beard card added flavor and character to stories about the likeable Aulai, but his dominating play on the field would become his trademark and legacy at BYU. Aulai and his fellow offensive linemen blocked for an offense that averaged 466 yards a game in 2006, good for fourth in the country. BYU finished the season with an 11-2 record and a 38-8 Las Vegas Bowl victory over the University of Oregon. Aulai allowed only one sack on the season, an amazing accomplishment considering the Cougar quarterbacks attempted 448 passes in 2006.

At the outset of the 2007 season, Aulai was selected as a team captain by his teammates. He and his fellow offensive linemen continued their strong play as the Cougars produced another 11-2 record and again won the Las Vegas Bowl, defeating the UCLA Bruins 17-16. Aulai continued to develop and perform well on the field, but he was also going through some changes away from the gridiron.

After taking over as head coach, Bronco Mendenhall began a

Photo Troy Verde/Total Blue Sports

tradition of holding several team firesides each football season. During these firesides, a few players were chosen to speak to local LDS congregations in the cities where the team was playing. One such fireside was held in San Diego the week of the Cougars' final 2007 regular season game against the San Diego State Aztecs. When Aulai got up and humbly spoke about his faith in Jesus Christ and his role as a disciple, many in the audience were surprised to learn that he was not a member of the LDS Church. In the preceding months, Aulai had experienced a spiritual awakening of sorts and the fireside talk was one of many steps he took as part of a spiritual journey that would dramatically change his life.

Although he still wasn't a member of the LDS faith, Aulai attended a singles ward with a few of his teammates, viewing it as a social function rather than a spiritual one. Over time that began to change. "After that I kind of developed a small testimony and it just started to grow from there," said Aulai. "I went to church with Ray [Feinga], Fui [Vakapuna] and Manase [Tonga], but it was more just to go to church. After going for a while with them, I really started to investigate the Church. I was like, 'Alright, let's see what the LDS faith is really about.' "

At BYU, Aulai roomed with a walk-on defensive tackle from San Bernardino by the name of Mark Fitu, who wasn't on the team very long due to injury. Fitu invited him to attend the priesthood session of General Conference in October, 2007.

"It all started with President Hinckley," Aulai recalled. "I went to his last priesthood session before he passed away. Mark was going and got me an extra ticket, and I really enjoyed that last priesthood session and will always remember that last talk he gave that day. The topic was anger, and I kid you not, I thought he was talking directly to me because I have a short temper. I'm pretty sure people remember that out on the football field." Soon, Aulai became more involved with the Church, even as a non-

Photo Troy Verde/Total Blue Sports

member.

"Then, and this is kind of funny, I became a home teacher and I wasn't even a member of the Church," Aulai explained with a laugh. "Can you believe that? I was in this single student ward at BYU, the 136th Ward. I was going there for a little bit and they asked me if I wanted to be a home teacher, and I was like, 'What the heck is a home teacher?' After they told me about it I was like, 'Yeah, I'll do it.' So I was a home teacher for a little while, and after doing all that and going to church and doing everything that the Church teaches, like read and pray and all that, something happened on July 12th, 2008." That was the day that Aulai was baptized a member of the Church of Jesus Christ of Latter-day Saints.

"My uncle Tupule Poloa, who was in the bishopric up here in Salt Lake City, is the one that baptized me," said Aulai. "I didn't do it because of some girl or for my friends. I did it because I wanted to, and I'm not going to lie, there were so many people that attended my baptism. It was like a stake conference because that's how many people were there. There were so many players from the team that were there, all the coaches were there and even Tom Holmoe was there. All the people from my singles ward were there, and they had to open up the overflow for the gym up because there were so many people there."

Having his BYU coaches there for his baptism was a special experience for Aulai. "One thing I remember was Coach Tidwell was so happy to see that I was baptized that he was lost for words," Aulai recalled. "He didn't say much, but you could just see it in his face, and Coach Reynolds was there and he was so happy, too. All the coaches were just so happy. They really didn't say much, but you could see it on their faces. Just by the look on their faces, that said everything. Coach Kaufusi never would have thought that day would come, but things happen for a reason.

"You know, looking back from the time I played football at El

Camino Junior College to now, my life has changed drastically. There has been such a change with me and I'm pretty sure you can tell from when you used to talk to me back then to when you talk to me now. Even Coach Kaufusi has seen the change in me. He said it's night and day from the Sete that first came to BYU to the Sete now after BYU. He said it's night and day, and I saw the change too."

In the year following his baptism, Aulai again donned a helmet and pads as a member of the Utah Valley Thunder of the American Indoor Football Association, along with former BYU players Chris Bolden and Dustin Rykert. The team finished the season 11-3 and made the Western Division playoffs, but the highlight of 2009 for Sete Aulai came away from the football field. He met a girl from Washington, and the two were sealed in the Seattle Washington Temple in November of 2009.

"I married a palagi [Caucasian] girl from Seattle named Megan Smart. She's not only smart but beautiful," said a smiling Aulai. Shortly after being sealed to his wife, Aulai began a new career as a police officer for the city of West Valley, Utah. Looking back, Aulai sees the subtle influences that directed him towards the life he now lives.

"You know, there was this Samoan kid from L.A. who had overcome his old ways, and even my parents have seen the change in me," Aulai said. "They've see how my life has changed and the man that I've become, and it's because of my experiences at BYU and the gospel. It's had such an influence on me and even before I was baptized, the influence of the gospel had an influence on me because of the example of the players on the team. I saw these really good football players who were tough and dominated on the field but were returned missionaries. Those off-the-field experiences had an effect on my life.

"You know, I truly believe there was a greater reason why I came to BYU other than just playing football. At the time when I first committed to play football at BYU I didn't see it, but now I do. I have no doubt in my mind that someone influenced me to come to BYU because of that greater reason. I am truly lucky that I've had the opportunity to come here. When Bronco offered me that scholarship, there was no doubt in my mind that I was supposed to come here. I knew BYU was an LDS college, but that didn't matter to me.

"Something inside me told me that I needed to come here, and so when Bronco offered me that scholarship I committed. When someone says there is more to BYU than football, I know that's true. I didn't go on to the NFL, but there was something else in store for me and that's the reason why I feel I was supposed to go to BYU. Looking back, it's pretty clear what those reasons were and I'm blessed and grateful for that more than I could ever say."

ROBBIE BOSCO

Robbie Bosco's decision to play football for BYU yielded a national championship, and yet that wasn't even the most momentous thing to happen to him because of his choice. Instead of spending four or five years at BYU, he has spent the better part of the last 31 years at the university, and has found happiness through his membership in the Church of Jesus Christ of Latter-day Saints.

Bosco grew up in Roseville, California, located near Sacramento. The youngest of four children, he has two sisters and a brother. His parents belonged to different faiths, and so Bosco and his siblings were never raised in any particular church.

"My mom's a member of the Church," Bosco said. "Her maiden name is Woodruff, so I'm the great, great grandson of Wilford Woodruff, which, to me growing up, didn't mean anything. Never thought, 'That's the prophet,' or anything like that."

Meanwhile, his dad's side of the family is staunch Catholic. His parents didn't put any pressure on the children to join any church.

"I wasn't a real big churchgoer," said Bosco. "We'd go to

Easter and go to Christmas [services], but I remember they'd always want me to go to Mutual whether it was just to play basketball or just to kind of hang out, but I just never wanted to do that kind of stuff either and never got into scouting and stuff like that."

A self-described "homebody to the max," Bosco may not have been interested in LDS activities, but he wasn't averse to the Church.

"I really didn't know a ton about it at all, and so I just knew a little about it," said Bosco. "My mom taught me a lot about it and things like that. Always had good feelings of it though. She could have told me any story, and I never doubted anything she ever told me about the Mormon Church, whether it was the Joseph Smith story or we have a Savior or anything like that, so I never had doubts of any of that stuff."

While he wasn't overly interested in outside activities, Bosco did have a love for football. His high school team ran a wishbone offense, which, with its heavy emphasis on running the ball, was hardly ideal for a quarterback that dreamed of throwing the ball.

In fact, according to Bosco, if his team threw the ball five times in a game those days, they were throwing it too much. But, things began to change. His coach was nice enough and smart enough, he said, to let them open the offense up and throw the ball more. Now that he was free to put up big passing stats, Bosco made a lot of all-Northern California teams.

Even more important, colleges began to take notice. That included pass-happy BYU.

In a bit of a coincidence, and maybe even fortuity, the man in charge of recruiting Northern California for BYU was defensive line coach Tom Ramage. Ramage had actually gone to school with Bosco's parents in Price, Utah.

As it turned out, Bosco had some interest in BYU as well thanks to a Cougar game he caught on national TV in 1979. The

Cougars were playing San Diego State on the road, and BYU quarterback Marc Wilson's first three passes were all touchdowns. The boys in blue came away with a 63-14 victory, and Bosco came away impressed and intrigued.

"I mean, it was just incredible, and so I always thought, 'Well, that would be a great place to go and play football.'"

His senior year in high school was also the year that Jim McMahon set 32 NCAA records and tied two more.

"Who doesn't want to go there if you throw the ball?" Bosco thought.

Beyond the fact that BYU threw the ball a lot, Bosco didn't know much about BYU. Every summer his family would go to Price for summer vacation to visit relatives, and would drive through Provo to get there. In addition, he went to a basketball camp on campus once, but that was it.

Meanwhile, Bosco was being recruited by a number of other schools, some of which were smaller schools or ones that didn't throw the ball much. He was, however, offered by San Diego State and Cal. Bosco was particularly intrigued by SDSU because of head coach Doug Scovil, who had previously served as BYU's offensive coordinator and quarterback coach. He figured that Scovil was the one who made BYU's quarterbacks who they were.

The University of Washington also showed interest in Bosco, but he turned the school down and focused on BYU, SDSU and Cal.

"I had interest in all three, and deep down BYU was where I wanted to go because that's where the so-called QB factory was, and they were the ones throwing for all the yards and things like that," he said.

However, he was hesitant to commit to BYU because the Cougars were also looking at a "hotshot" quarterback in Southern California, Sean Salisbury. Bosco felt that BYU was recruiting Salisbury a little bit harder, and that Salisbury would get the first shot if the two of them went to BYU. He said that he wasn't afraid of competition, but felt it wouldn't be in his best interest to go to BYU if Salisbury did. So, Bosco decided to let Salisbury decide first, and then he would make his own decision.

Ramage was in Roseville for about two weeks waiting for him to make a decision, Bosco recalled with a laugh. One day while Bosco was in school, Ramage tapped on his classroom window. Bosco went outside, at which point Ramage informed him that Salisbury had committed to USC.

It was time for Bosco to pull the trigger.

He immediately went and called his dad and told him that he wanted to be a BYU Cougar.

"When I decided to come here ... I never thought once, 'Oh, I'm going to a Mormon school, I'm going to a private school' or anything like that. I'm going there to play football, and that was my ultimate thing is to play football there."

Arriving at BYU in 1981, he was teammates with a couple legendary quarterbacks in Jim McMahon and Steve Young. He didn't spend much time with McMahon aside from playing golf with him, but he did become good friends with Young.

"He was just a year older than I was, and he was an amazing example too," Bosco said about Young. "He would have me go speak with him at firesides. We'd hang out a lot more together. And so when you're surrounded by great people, you do great things, and I think that's what invites the Spirit, and it was always there. It wasn't like I'm walking around thinking, 'I've got the Spirit with me,' you know. But it was just like you felt you wanted to do good things, you wanted to do good things for other people and things like that, so that was a great experience being around Steve."

Bosco may not have been actively seeking out the gospel, but the gospel had found him, and so his path to conversion had started.

BYU QB Robbie Bosco   Photo George Gojkovich/Getty

While growing up, none of Bosco's friends went to church. But as his friends at BYU went to church, he figured he should be going too instead of staying in the dorms by himself. He was greatly influenced by the support system he had in place in Provo, whether it was his friends, roommates, teammates or the overall environment at BYU. He credited his roommate, fellow quarterback Blaine Fowler, with getting the ball rolling by having missionaries come over to their dorm room, while other friends were a positive influence on him and set great examples.

Bosco's coaches were good examples as well, especially head coach LaVell Edwards.

"Coach Edwards gave me a blessing one time – this was when I was a member – and how many head coaches can do that, or have the time to do that, LDS or not? I mean, he was just a genuine person, and him and his wife Patti were really big influences in my life also."

As Bosco attended church, he learned more about the doctrines his mother had shared with him when he was younger. He said that because of how strongly he felt the Spirit, he knew the Church was true. Bosco "just knew this was it. I knew that was the right thing to do, and to get baptized was what I wanted to do."

He had been to other churches in the past, but nothing ever really seemed real to him, he said.

"There's a lot of good things about those places, but nothing struck me like it did here and what it was like to go to church and to have this many friends that went to church," said Bosco.

On February 21, 1982, during the second semester of his freshman year, Bosco was baptized into the Church of Jesus Christ of Latter-day Saints by Chris Germann, a kicker on the football team.

"I don't have any miraculous story that I read the Book of Mormon and it was just unbelievable, but I just never doubted that this was what I needed to be, where I needed to be, and what I needed to do," said Bosco. "So everything kind of fell into place for me perfectly, I think, especially now that I look back."

Not only did things fall into place spiritually for Bosco, but they also fell into place athletically. After redshirting in 1982 and backing up Young in 1983, he finally got his chance to shine in 1984 as the starting quarterback.

Following the likes of McMahon and Young was a daunting task, yet Bosco proved to be up to the task.

Prior to the start of Bosco's first season, his brother was always talking big – big as in undefeated. With the teams on the schedule, his brother would say, the Cougars could win it all.

But a perfect record and national title weren't necessarily on the Cougars' minds.

"No one even thought about that around here," said Bosco. "I mean, the highest ranked team I think we had before that probably was 7 or 8, and we had so many new guys."

And yet, the Cougars kept winning and winning as the season wore on. After a perfect regular season, the Cougars found themselves ranked first in the nation, and needed a bowl victory to clinch their first national championship.

Facing Michigan in the Holiday Bowl, however, the Cougars found themselves in peril. Bosco got beat up badly, suffering from hurt knee ligaments and cracked ribs. But what hurt the most was an ankle sprain. To make matters worse, the Wolverines led 17-10 in the fourth quarter.

After getting injured, Bosco went to the trainers and asked if he could get hurt worse if he continued to play.

"When they said no, I said, 'Let's go. Pick me up and let's just go.' And I don't know, I just had that attitude when I played that you just want to play. That's what we're here to do, we're here to play football, not try to stay out of games and be out of games."

So, Bosco made sure the trainers taped up his hurt knee tight enough and went back out onto the field. If there was any game that called for gutting through injuries, this was it, given everything that was on the line. Yet, Bosco said he would have likely returned to the field even if it was for some other less meaningful game.

"I always felt if you could walk, you could play."

But walking didn't come easy for Bosco thanks to his ankle. In fact, the coaches made a key change in order to keep him from having to continuously drop back to pass.

"We went in the shotgun, which I never had before, at all," said Bosco. "That was the first time we ever did it. And so, with those kind of changes, it was just major adrenaline pumping me through that game big time."

Bosco threw two fourth-quarter touchdowns, the last one coming with 1:23 left in the game, to give the Cougars a 24-17 victory. BYU had successfully completed a perfect season, and was the only undefeated team in 1984.

"That year was awesome," said Bosco.

It was also an opportunity to prove people wrong, as BYU became the only non-traditional power in college football to win a national championship in the modern era.

"If we would have lost one game that year, we would just kind of been like a bunch of other teams that played here," Bosco said. "And so by doing what we did, I think it puts us on that pedestal as far as the team aspect of it goes, and to have done something that no one else has ever done."

Of course, after a national championship in his first season as a starter, Bosco would be hard-pressed to top that.

Ever the optimist, Bosco's brother went to him and said he thought they could win it all again.

"And this time I'm like, 'Yeah, we could!' because we had a great team, we had a great team coming back and a lot of good players and it was just a matter of staying healthy and we had a shot to do it," Bosco said.

However, the Cougars weren't able to stay healthy.

"Injuries kind of killed us that year, but it was a fun year though," he said.

After losing to UCLA in the second game of the season, a Temple defender drilled Bosco in the shoulder with his helmet two games later. The hit tore all of the tendons in his shoulder, and for the remainder of the season, Bosco's arm would come out of his socket each time he threw.

"I'd kind of throw it, and always felt like I had to kind of tuck my shoulder a little bit," said Bosco. "I just couldn't just throw it like I used to throw it, so my arm just wasn't as good as it used to be."

And yet despite the injuries to him and others on offense, Bosco actually continued to amass big passing stats.

"The funny thing is my stats were better in every category, even interceptions. That's what kind of killed me," he said wryly. "When I say better, I threw more – not better [as in] less."

Indeed, except for throwing three fewer touchdowns, he actually increased his total completions, completion percentage, total yards, and yards per game.

The Cougars finished with an 11-3 record, with Bosco's only real disappointment being a shocking upset loss to an otherwise winless UTEP team.

Following a couple years in the NFL with the Green Bay Packers in which he never threw a pass, Bosco eventually found himself back at BYU. Starting in 1990 – Ty Detmer's Heisman season – Bosco coached BYU's quarterbacks. It was a job he would hold onto until 2003.

Since then he has worked as an administrator in BYU's athletics department, and has been involved primarily with fundraising. He also works with former athletes, getting them involved with reunions or tailgates at Cougar football games.

Robbie Bosco (6) with fellow BYU All-American quarterbacks Gifford Nielsen (14),
Jim McMahon (9) and Steve Young (8) at halftime of the BYU vs. Univ. of
Washington game in 2010

Photo Troy Verde/Total Blue Sports

"We want them to have that same feeling that they had when they were here," he said.

He also seeks to encourage them to give back to BYU, not just monetarily, but also with their time and service.

Bosco even stepped outside of his football expertise to coach BYU's women's golf team for one semester while the school sought to hire a more permanent coach.

"I loved doing that, and I'd do it again in a heartbeat. It was great."

Bosco said it seems like he's been at BYU most of his life, and he isn't wrong. Since he arrived at BYU in 1981, Bosco has spent all but about four years in Provo.

"I've had opportunities to go other places, and it always comes down to where do I want to raise my kids, and there's a lot of great places all over the country that you can raise kids just as good, but I think my wife and I always felt this was the place where we wanted to do it. We wanted to stay here and be a part of this university and the feeling that it gives us."

He recognizes how different his life would have been had he not chosen BYU all those years ago.

"First of all, I wouldn't have married my wife," he said.

Bosco met his wife at BYU after he converted, and they went on to have six kids, who are now between the ages of 14 and 22. He credited her with making it possible for him to succeed in various aspects of his life, whether it be football or in the Church.

Had he chosen to attend Cal or SDSU, Bosco's religious path would surely be very different as well.

"Honestly, with the influences I would have had at those places, I know for a fact I wouldn't have joined the Church my second semester, or in February during that year," he said. "It may have been just later down the road. But that's the beauty of this place right here that I think I love and all people that have ever come here have loved, is just what BYU represents, what

BYU is all about. You just cannot find this atmosphere anywhere else, not only with the athletes but also just the students, the faculty, the coaches. Everybody that surrounds this place does good things, is good."

Being at BYU taught Bosco a lesson about surrounding oneself with good people. It was something he observed LaVell Edwards do.

"He surrounded himself with great people and great coaches, and that's why I think he was so successful. And I think if we do that in life, if we can surround ourselves with great people, great things will happen to us and we'll want to keep doing great things."

Through his conversion, Bosco has also been able to serve as an example to others.

"As time has gone on, I think it's had a major impact on my family, especially those that are nonmembers," he said, singling out his nonmember father. "And the impact is kind of the good examples that our children are and how they've kind of grown up and kind of the choices that they've made in their lives."

Bosco himself has grown over the years as a member of the Church. He started out with a calling in the nursery, and has since served in young men's presidencies, elders quorum presidencies, a bishopric, as an executive secretary, and currently as a high councilman.

But beyond growing with various responsibilities and leadership positions, he has grown spiritually.

"In my 30 years of being a member now, I mean, I've grown as much in my last 10 years than I did my previous 15 – at least I hope I've just gotten a stronger and stronger testimony."

Through leading BYU to the national title in 1984, Bosco has also played a part in increasing the Church's visibility.

"Well at the time, I remember one of the General Authorities told me that it was like the highest baptizing year we've ever had," he said. "And so, athletics I think has a great impact on people, and I think that's part of what we're trying to do now is get out there in front of people. BYUtv is a major impact in what we do and what we want to be about."

A lot of good things came about because BYU was in the national limelight, Bosco said, as suddenly people became interested in what the school was all about. Not only that, but people also became curious about the Book of Mormon and the Church of Jesus Christ of Latter-day Saints, things that they possibly hadn't heard much about previously.

"Anytime you can do something positive, especially in the athletic field, I just think it's a great impact on just people in general," said Bosco. "Whether they're members or not, I think it has an impact on everybody."

.

8

SHAUN NUA

As a young boy on the island of Tutuila, American Samoa, young Shaun Nua often trekked through the ferns and banyan palms of the tropical forest with his father and uncle as they hunted wild pigs for their family dinner. On one of those hunting trips, Shaun had an experience that remains etched in his memory to this day. Shaun and his uncle spotted a wild boar and quickly used a rope to snag one of its hind legs as it attempted to flee. As the boar squealed and struggled frantically to escape, young Shaun knew the animal needed to be restrained before it could be killed.

After a command from his uncle, Shaun set his fear aside and approached the boar to further restrain it. As he slowly moved closer, the boar suddenly broke loose from the rope. The terror in Shaun's eyes told the whole story. Paralyzed by fear, he could only watch as the angry boar charged him. He stood motionless with eyes wide open as he was hit in the chest by the full force of the charging boar, sending him backwards through the air. He hit the ground with a thud and began to cry. The pig won the battle that day, but Shaun would grow in both strength and stature. He would eventually be on the delivering end of countless collisions, but they take place on the football field.

Shaun played football for Tafuna High School in American Samoa. After completing his senior year for the Warriors he was named all-league at defensive end, but attention from college recruiters was scant. Visits by coaches from the mainland were understandably rare given the considerable distance and expense required to see a Samoan player in action. Without a Division I scholarship available, Nua accepted an offer from Eastern Arizona College to play at the junior college level, allowing him an opportunity to pursue his dream of one day playing in the NFL.

With a total land area of just 76 square miles, the tiny islands of America Samoa were the only home that the 18-year-old Nua had ever known. The scholarship to EAC and a new life in the high desert of the Southwest presented an array of possibilities, challenges and opportunities. In the summer of 2000 Nua began his new life, traveling 4,000 miles from his island home to the small town of Thatcher, Arizona where he would play for the Gila Monsters.

Upon arriving in Thatcher to begin both his football career and college studies, the brawny 6-foot-6-inch Samoan stood out among the locals. Although American Samoa is a territory of the United States, Arizona seemed like a foreign country in many ways. With just 10 inches of annual rainfall, the desert climate in Thatcher and the surrounding Gila Valley bore a stark contrast to the lush, green, tropical climate that Nua knew back in Pago Pago, the capital of American Samoa. Thatcher was a dusty town of 5,000 residents with a single stoplight, a few gas stations and what seemed to be a Mormon church building on every corner. The latter was something that Nua was actually used to seeing back home.

First visited by Mormon missionaries in 1843, American Samoa has one of the highest concentrations of LDS Church members in the world. Shaun was not a member of the LDS faith growing up,

BYU DL Shaun Nua makes a tackle   Photo Troy Verde/Total Blue Sports

but most of his friends were, and through them he was somewhat familiar with the Church and its unique culture. Like American Samoa, Thatcher has a long Mormon history dating back to the 1800s. The town was first settled by pioneer John Moody in 1881, and roughly one quarter of the town's residents are members of the Church of Jesus Christ of Latter-day Saints. In fact, Eastern Arizona College itself was originally founded by the LDS Church in 1888 as the St. Joseph Stake Academy.

The LDS Church did not play a significant role in Nua's life at the time, but it was always in the background throughout his youth in American Samoa and again in Arizona. That background presence would continue in Nua's life as he moved forward.

At 6 feet 6 inches and 270 pounds, Nua was remarkably quick, and it wasn't long before he was dominating at the junior college level. He was named to the ACCAC All-Conference team as a freshman in 2000 and then earned All-American honors as a sophomore in 2001. The recruiting attention intensified during his second year at EAC, and Nua had numerous colleges in pursuit throughout the season, including USC, Arizona State, BYU, Arizona and Wisconsin.

Paul Tidwell was the BYU coach assigned to recruit the state of Arizona, and he had strong connections to both the state and EAC. Tidwell was the head coach of the Gila Monsters from 1995 to 1997 and he was immensely popular in the community after leading the team to its first winning season in 26 years. Tidwell was also recruiting Nua's EAC teammate, Walt Williams, who was considered by many to be the top junior college cornerback recruit in the country. Williams took an official recruiting visit to BYU on November 17, 2001, and Tidwell convinced Nua to come along.

Nua and Williams were on hand that night in Provo as the Cougars defeated in-state rival Utah in front of a sold-out stadium of 66,149 fans. The Cougars' victory was sealed when junior running back Luke Staley left Ute defenders in the dust, racing down the sideline for a 30-yard touchdown run with 1:16 remaining. Times were good in Provo and with a sparkling 11-0 record, the Cougars were ranked seventh in the country. Nua was impressed with the team and loved his visit. He still had other offers on the table and several schools were pushing him to take an official visit, but Nua had made up his mind. Shortly after his visit, Nua verbally committed to BYU head coach Gary Crowton.

Nua did have some knowledge of BYU prior to his official recruiting visit. Kalani Sitake, an assistant coach at EAC, had played for BYU the prior season and spoke highly of the program. Sitake would join Nua in Provo the following season as a graduate assistant for the Cougars. Nua also had friends back in American Samoa who attended school at BYU.

When asked in 2002 about signing with BYU and agreeing to live by the school's honor code, Nua said, "I'm not LDS, but it's not hard for me. Back home, there's a lot of LDS people and so most of my friends, not all of them, but most of them are LDS. BYU's culture is the LDS Church and where I'm from there are mostly LDS people. Also there's a lot of Polynesians here and that makes it much easier.

"In my high school senior year, I heard about BYU, but not a lot," Nua explained. "I heard about the LDS Church more than BYU. But when I got to Arizona, that's when BYU came in. Hearing about BYU being an LDS school and thinking, 'That's where all my friends went. Let's go check out where all my friends went to back home.'" Nua made his commitment official on signing day in February, 2002. Upon finishing his associate's degree at EAC, he made the move to Provo.

Nua performed well on the field as a junior in 2002. He played in all 12 games and finished the year with 20 tackles, including eight for a loss, and was second on team with four sacks. Away

Photo Troy Verde/Total Blue Sports

from the field, he was comfortable at BYU and was thoroughly enjoying his experience as a non-LDS athlete at the Mormon-sponsored university. Nua quickly developed a close friendship with his BYU teammates, both members and non-members of the LDS faith. He especially liked the Polynesian influence at BYU and cited it as a factor in his decision to commit to the Cougars.

"It makes a big difference," Nua said. "I like being around people who understand me and know how I am. There's no other place but here that's like that. I think it's the church culture being the same as the Poly culture here. LDS people have so much loyalty, just like the Polynesian people. They always stick together."

Nua's friend and teammate Manaia Brown, who began his career at Nebraska before transferring to BYU, also cited the Polynesian influence at BYU as a factor in his choice to play there. "I'm more comfortable here at BYU [than Nebraska] because I don't have to explain to anyone that I'm not Hawaiian or Mexican or a big Indian. Everyone knows about the different Polynesians here. Plus, we've got a big Polynesian community here at this school with members and non-members."

Nua also enjoyed the LDS influence at BYU and saw it as a positive aspect of playing there. "My experience here is awesome. I'm around good people, man. LDS people are good people. There's no pressure; just the missionaries who come every day," Nua joked.

"They knock on the door and I say, 'Hey, I gotta go to work.' It's not a bad thing and I don't feel any pressure. I think Gabe Reid and those guys sent them," added a laughing Nua. "I love it at BYU with all the Polys. I just love it. I don't think I was meant to go anywhere else."

After wrapping up spring practice in 2003, when he saw limited action due to a knee injury, Nua had high expectations for his senior season. However, those expectations soon lay in ruins after a meeting with new defensive coordinator Bronco Mendenhall that felt like the pummeling he took from the wild boar as a young boy. Mendenhall openly acknowledged Nua's tremendous talent, but felt he was undisciplined and didn't work hard enough. The coach told Nua that because of his lack of effort and discipline, he wouldn't play a down in the 2003 season. Devastated by what he heard, a tearful Nua asked Mendenhall what he had to do. Mendenhall told him it would come down to one thing: effort.

Not willing to spend his senior season on the bench, Nua responded with a renewed level of dedication and focus. He spent that offseason working on his game and his conditioning and didn't let up while redshirting during the 2003 season. After a year of maximum effort to convince Coach Mendenhall that his dedication was where it needed to be, Nua was rewarded with the playing time he desired. As a starter at defensive end in 2004, he had 34 tackles, including eight for a loss, and led the Cougars with six sacks. Nua was named to the All-Mountain West Conference second team, and the following April was selected by the Pittsburgh Steelers in the seventh round of the 2005 NFL draft.

In his first year with the Steelers, Nua reached the pinnacle of what he believed life could offer. As a rookie, Nua was part of the 2005 Steelers squad that beat the Seattle Seahawks to win Super Bowl XL.

"Here I am, a kid from Samoa, playing in the biggest football arena in the world," said Nua. "I was living what I thought was my dream. I had reached my final goal. I won a Super Bowl my rookie year and thought, 'Man, is this it?'

"It wasn't what I thought it would be when I was a kid. I mean, I was on the field and on the sidelines as an NFL player and we won a Super Bowl. It just wasn't what I thought. When it was all said and done, it really helped me to see what BYU was really all about."

Photo Troy Verde/Total Blue Sports

Growing up in American Samoa, Nua and his family didn't have much and lived off the land. After his three-year stint in the NFL and a Super Bowl victory, Nua found that the dream he once had was unfulfilling and didn't bring the happiness he expected.

"I learned that money will not make you happy, that fame is overrated and it makes you forget who you are and where you come from," said Nua with a serious tone. "It made me realize that there was something more valuable out there than fame, money and football. Man, it made me think and finally realize all those things that Bronco Mendenhall had been teaching me when I was a player at BYU. It finally all came together."

After playing for the Steelers from 2005 to 2007, Nua played a year with the Buffalo Bills in 2008. In 2009, he made his way back to BYU as a graduate assistant coaching offense. He was later moved to the defensive side after Coach Jaime Hill was fired five games into the 2010 season. Nua was thrilled to be back on the defensive side of the ball where he played at BYU. He was excited to share the knowledge he had gained while playing in a 3-4 defense under Pittsburgh defensive line coach John Mitchell, who is currently the longest tenured member of the Steelers' staff with 18 years of NFL experience.

However, the chance to share what he had learned in the NFL was just one of the benefits Nua found in coming back to BYU. On September 29, 2010, Nua entered the waters of baptism and became a member of the Church of Jesus Christ of Latter-day Saints.

"It's been nine years since the time I first stepped foot on campus to the day I got baptized," said Nua shortly after his baptism. "What influenced me was I wanted to be happy. When I left for the NFL, I was happy but I wasn't completely happy. Something was missing inside. I'm not bashing on any other church and I think all other churches are good, but I just felt peace and happiness in this church. It took a long time, and it wasn't like I wasn't happy with my old church – I just felt more comfortable with this church and I believe in it. When I finally investigated the Church on my own, I realized things were different and saw for myself the fullness. Before I wasn't complete, and right now this is the most complete I've ever been.

"When I first came here to BYU, I came here for football, but what I found was something bigger. My path is kind of funny and I definitely found something bigger than just football through BYU. Now I'm coaching here and I love being around these kids. One day I would like to take everything I've gained from this experience and go back home to Samoa and help the little kids live the dream I once had."

While playing for the Cougars, Nua grew very close to Jim Hamblin, a staff member at the Student Athlete Academic Center. After deciding to join the Church, Nua asked Hamblin to perform the baptism.

"Hamblin and I have been friends since I was here," Nua explained. "If you go to his office and sit there the whole day, it's like a therapy session. You'll see members of the Church, nonmembers, white people, black people, Tongans, Samoans, Fijians, and all kinds of people will be in his office. He never forced me to become a member, but if I had a question he would answer it. He's a good friend and a good person and when I asked him to baptize me, he answered the call. He's a great-hearted guy and helps out all the kids from all sports. I wouldn't have wanted anybody else to baptize me."

The baptismal service was a special occasion and Nua invited some of the people who influenced him at BYU to participate at his baptism. "Coach Reynolds gave me the gift of the Holy Ghost," Nua said. "He's another special man and a great influence. With Coach Tidwell, it was kind of a last-minute thing, and I was thinking, 'Who better to give the talk on [baptism] than the person who brought me here?' Coach Tidwell is the one that

Photo Troy Verde/Total Blue Sports

found me and recruited me, and so I picked him to give the talk on baptism. He's a great man and it's really because of him that I'm even here."

Meanwhile, Nua chose to have fellow graduate assistant Kelly Poppinga give the talk on the Holy Ghost at his baptism. "Kelly Poppinga is another person that I worked with and answered a lot of my questions," Nua said. "Last year when I was a G.A., we both would stay up late talking. We would get up early and talk some more. I had so many questions and he became a close friend of mine and is one of the best friends I've ever had."

Many of Nua's family members and friends attended his baptism and BYU president Cecil O. Samuelson was also there. "I didn't think there was going to be that many people there because it was such short notice," said Nua. "My parents made it here from back home in Samoa, and there were just a lot of people there. It was better than winning the Super Bowl. I was happy and I was on cloud nine and it's hard to explain. I wouldn't trade it for any Super Bowl ring and would give one away in a heartbeat to find what I've found.

"In fact, I did give my Super Bowl ring away to my dad the first day I got it," continued Nua. "I really don't care about things like that and would never trade this experience at BYU and joining the Church for anything in the world. A Super Bowl and a ring is something you can give away, but this experience is something you just can't trade for anything. There is no comparison between being baptized into the Church and winning the Super Bowl. I wouldn't trade being baptized for any Super Bowl ring. I'm really happy now. There is not even any comparison to finding the true religion. There is nothing better than that."

After completing his third year on the BYU coaching staff in 2011, Shaun Nua was hired as the defensive line coach at the Naval Academy in January of 2012.

"Shaun is a bright and enthusiastic coach and I'm very excited to have him join our staff," said Navy head coach Ken Niumatalolo, who is also LDS, in a press release. "He is a man of character and coaches with a great deal of passion. I went to BYU last spring to watch a couple of spring practices and he immediately caught my attention with the way he coached. He will be a great asset."

"I am very excited to be at Navy," said Nua. "I have so much respect for these young men and what they do here at the Naval Academy and what they are going to do after graduation. I am fired up about having a role in helping these young men progress on the football field and I am very grateful that Coach Niumatalolo has given me this opportunity."

"Shaun is an exceptional coach and an exceptional person," said Brigham Young head coach Bronco Mendenhall. "He has an outstanding defensive mind blended with great optimism, and he is an excellent teacher who cares for the players in his charge. Our players and coaches are sorry to see him leave, but excited for him and his opportunity at Navy. Shaun has a very bright future in the coaching profession."[1]

KRESIMIR COSIC

Kresimir Cosic was born in Zagreb, Yugoslavia (now Croatia), on November 26, 1948. He was raised in the small town of Zadar on the coast of the Adriatic Sea, where his father worked in the hotel industry. From an early age, "Kreso" (as he was often called) had no intention of following his father's career path. "As a child he never cared much for academics, he just loved basketball," daughter Ana explained in a 2012 interview with Total Blue Sports. "As soon as he would wake up in the morning until he would go to bed, he would just be shooting hoops."

Very tall for his age, young Kreso was convinced that he would one day be a basketball star. Convincing the other kids in his Zadar neighborhood that he would one day achieve his dream was not an easy task. "The kids used to make fun of him because he was very scrawny," Ana said. "He was very, very skinny. They called him 'vein,' like the vein in your arm, because of how skinny he was. They used to make fun of him. 'You're never going to be a player; you're never going to be able to play basketball, what is wrong with you?' Later, of course, I guess he showed them." Showed them he did. Ignoring the skeptics and mockery, Kreso relentlessly pursued his dream. At the age of 16, he became the youngest member of the Yugoslavian national basketball team.

Within two years of making the national team, Kreso had grown to 6 feet 11 inches and became a dominant force in European basketball. Only 18 years old, Cosic had already been named to the All-European team, led his local team to three Yugoslavian championships, and won a silver medal at the world championships and a gold medal at the Mediterranean Games. The young Yugoslavian star then made his big splash on the international stage as Yugoslavia shocked the world by beating the Soviet Union in the semifinals of the 1968 Olympic Games in Mexico, ultimately winning a silver medal. Looking back on that time, Cosic explained that he was already one of the top five players in Europe as an 18-year-old and he was looking for a greater challenge. "I was 18...and I knew that was the top for Europe," Cosic said. "There was nothing more for me to do."[1]

In the months preceding the Olympic Games, Kreso was playing in tournaments for a European club team. One of his teammates, 6-foot-9-inch Finnish center Veikko Vainio, had enrolled at Brigham Young University the previous season. The NCAA granted foreign basketball players amateur status at that time, making them eligible to participate in college athletics. Vainio knew the young Yugoslavian star was looking for a greater challenge on the court and encouraged Kreso to join him at BYU.

Vainio also told BYU assistant basketball coach Pete Witbeck about Cosic in the summer of 1968. After watching Cosic's Olympic performance in October of that year, Witbeck and BYU head coach Stan Watts were convinced they should try to bring the Yugoslavian star to Provo. Witbeck would later recall, "I thought, 'Wow, there's three conference championships right there.' "[2]

However, this would not be a normal recruiting process. Witbeck once described it as a "cloak-and-dagger adventure."[3]

Young Kresimir Cosic grabs a rebound   Photo KK Zadar

The recruitment was complicated by the fact that Yugoslavia was a communist country and Cosic would be forced to defect from his homeland in order to play basketball in the United States. In spite of the challenges and risks, Witbeck pushed forward. He first asked Vainio to pass along his business card to Cosic. He then secured the help of a translator and began writing letters to Cosic once a week, inviting him to continue his basketball career in Provo. Witbeck followed up on the letters with monthly phone calls to Cosic, also through an interpreter. After a year of letters and late night phone calls and messages from Witbeck, Kreso was convinced that BYU could provide the challenge he was seeking. While playing in a tournament in Italy in 1969, Cosic defected from Yugoslavia, using a plane ticket Witbeck had sent him to leave his team and fly to the United States.

When Cosic finally arrived at the Salt Lake City airport at midnight, he was greeted by Witbeck and the interpreter. As the three men drove to Provo, Witbeck began explaining the BYU honor code to his new recruit, and it didn't go well. Cosic was surprised and concerned by what he was hearing. "We went through all of the rules," Witbeck said. "When I got through the last one, at about Point of the Mountain, he said, 'Stop the car!' I thought, 'Well, that was a good trip. We had him for all of 20 minutes.'" After another 10 minutes of questions and answers regarding the BYU honor code and lifestyle, Cosic said, "Coach, what do you do at BYU for fun?"[4]

Former BYU English tutor Katherine Farmer remembered Cosic's dismay upon learning about the strict honor code. "When he got here they seemingly didn't prepare him terribly well for the nature of what our school was."[5] Cosic was also disappointed to learn that NCAA regulations didn't allow freshmen to play varsity basketball, so he was relegated to playing for the freshman team his first year in Provo. Kreso didn't disappoint, averaging 17 points and 13 rebounds, but the freshman team did not offer the level of competition he was seeking when he decided to defect from his homeland and come to the United States.

After a frustrating first season in Provo, Cosic had decided to leave Provo and return home. Close friend Christina Nibley Mincek recalled the experience. "He did not tell anybody, including me, until I was at his house studying...and he was packing. He told me then, 'I'm going home. I told you I wasn't going to stay.' He left. He went to the airport and I thought he was gone and I was very sad."[6]

Mincek was relieved when Cosic returned just three hours later, telling her that he "didn't make it." He explained that members of the BYU basketball coaching staff had learned of his plan to leave and were waiting to intercept him when he arrived at the airport. After a conversation with the coaches, Kreso changed his mind and decided to remain in Provo.

With his newfound resolve to stay in Provo, Cosic began preparing for his first year of varsity basketball for the Cougars. Upon watching Cosic in the Olympics, Witbeck had predicted he would bring conference championships to the Cougars if they could sign him. Kreso did not disappoint. On top of Western Athletic Conference championships in 1971 and 1972, Cosic led the Cougars to the NCAA Regionals both years. He was named to the All-WAC team three consecutive seasons and was the conference Most Valuable Player in 1973. Cosic also became the first foreign basketball player to be named All-American, earning the honor in both 1972 and 1973.

The 6-foot-11-inch Cosic played center for the Cougars, but the fans who watched him remember how the big man with number 11 on his jersey dribbled, passed and shot like a guard. Taking time out to play for his national team in the 1972 Olympics, Kreso continued to impress the basketball world with his unique skill set. UTEP head coach and eventual Basketball Hall of Fame inductee Don Haskins was an assistant coach for the U.S. squad in

Cosic in action   Photo Doug Martin/BYU

the 1972 Olympics in Munich, Germany. After watching Kreso's performance in the '72 games, Haskins called Cosic "the best center in the Olympics."[7]

Cosic's Olympic performance was no surprise to Haskins, who coached in the WAC. His UTEP Miner team began a five-year home-court winning streak upon joining the WAC. That streak came to an end in 1973 on a last-second shot by Cosic. Down 55-54 with 25 seconds to play, BYU head coach Glenn Potter told his team that whoever had the ball with five seconds left would shoot it. Not surprisingly, Kreso was the player with the ball in his hands. In spite of being 25 feet from the hoop and double-teamed, Cosic launched a shot, sinking it to give the Cougars a 56-55 victory. "The way I've been shooting," Cosic said at the time, "I figured a 25-footer under pressure was safer than a five-foot pass."[8]

Cosic led the Cougars to great success on the court, but was sometimes scolded by Watts for dribbling and passing the ball too much. Like most coaches, Watts wanted his centers in the paint and his guards handling the ball. Recalling the discussions with Coach Watts, Cosic displayed his famous sense of humor, explaining that people always think "the short guys are the smart ones who think and the tall guys are the dumb ones who run and jump." Despite the stereotypes, Kreso saw no reason why he couldn't play like a point guard. "I saw no reason because I thought I had a great view from up at 6-11, I could see it much better than them, and from there I could develop anything."[9]

Cosic would finish his BYU career with 1,512 points, currently 13th best all-time and the best of any player who played only three seasons. His career scoring average of 19.2 points per game remains fourth-best in school history, and his three-year total of 919 career rebounds is second all-time.

Cosic found the on-court challenge he was seeking at BYU, but he also grew tremendously away from the basketball court. Cosic developed a close friendship with BYU religion and philosophy professor Truman Madsen and his wife Ann. Cosic gave Truman the nickname of "Boss" and the two would remain close friends for the rest of their lives. While in his second year at BYU, the friendship blossomed and Kreso opened up to Madsen. Kreso told his friend about a dream he had as a young boy which played a key role in his decision to play basketball for the Cougars.

"He saw himself in America, and that he was involved in a great athletic contest and that he was playing in the largest facility in the United States," Madsen said. "Well he remembered that. He came at the invitation of Stan Watts, then the head coach. Watts showed him the field house that would hold eight or ten thousand. 'Is this the largest basketball facility in the United States?' 'No.' And that troubled him a little, but before he finished his career, the Marriott Center was built and it was, at the time, the largest facility in the United States."[10]

Kreso's dream in which he saw himself playing in the largest basketball arena in the United States was fulfilled. Kreso was also widely credited with attracting the 22,700 fans to fill that arena. As Coach Watts told Croatian journalist Slavko Cvitkovic, "The saying around town was that I built the Marriott Center, Willard Marriott paid for it and Cosic filled it."[11]

Cosic also developed a close friendship with renowned BYU religion professor Hugh Nibley. Kreso had heard that Nibley had insights into the spiritual purposes of dreams, so Kresimir stopped by his office to learn more and a friendship soon followed. As Church News writer Shaun Stahle observed in 2006, the two friends would often create quite a sight as they crossed campus together — Brother Nibley standing at 5 feet 7 inches, dwarfed by Kresimir's 6-foot-11-inch height.[12] Cosic soon began meeting with Nibley on a frequent basis to learn more about the Church of Jesus Christ of Latter-day Saints.

As he learned more about the Church, Kreso was reminded of

spiritual teachings he had learned from his mother and grandmother. "Within my heart, there began to burn familiarities — feelings that I had known as a child," Cosic said. "The comfort and peace of eternal truths — truths I had been taught by my mother and by my grandmother, for under communism it was the women who kept the faith alive."[13]

Hugh Nibley's wife Phyllis witnessed Cosic's conversion process and saw the remarkable changes that took place. "He really had a deep and profound testimony of the gospel and it changed his whole life," she said.[14] Convinced that what he was learning was true, Cosic decided to be baptized a member of the Church of Jesus Christ of Latter-day Saints.

Cosic later described his conversion to the gospel of Jesus Christ in an interview for the New Era magazine. "I had never heard about the Church before I came here," he said. "In Yugoslavia most of the young people are completely atheistic, and that's the way I lived. When I came to Provo I didn't change. I was an atheist for two years while I was in Provo. Nobody was farther from becoming a Mormon than I was. I just lived my way, and people lived their way. I obeyed all the rules of BYU, tried to be as good as I could, and tried to play ball and do my studying and other things. When I was a junior, I decided to figure out a few things. I had things I wanted to know.

"I didn't decide to join the Church because of any one thing. There were some things that I wanted to know. I had a few questions that no one could answer. It just happened. We as Mormons believe in personal things everyone can know by himself. It all depends on how bad you want to know something. That's the whole point. If we have a desire in the Church to know something, we will know it; there's no question about that. If something is really bothering you, you probably go to somebody for advice. If it's football you want to know about—what kind of a play you are going to play—you can ask me, and I don't have any idea. I just can't help. It's the same if you're going to the wrong church. They can't give you an answer. So you ask, and find out, and you join the true church. So I just decided to join the Church."[15]

In November of 1971, a small group of friends gathered in the basement of the LDS Tabernacle on Temple Square in Salt Lake City for the baptismal service of Kresimir Cosic. Cosic chose the location and requested a small service to minimize public attention. In the days preceding the baptismal service, the sisters responsible for the baptismal clothing felt prompted to sew an extra long baptismal outfit. When they saw the 6-foot-11-inch Cosic, they knew the reason for the prompting.[16] Cosic was baptized by his close friend Hugh Nibley. Their friendship would continue as Kreso joined the Nibley family for their weekly family home evening throughout the remainder of his stay in Provo.

Cosic had studied the Book of Mormon and it was an important factor in his conversion process. Asked about the Book of Mormon, he said, "It's certainly the best book I have ever read. There's no question about that. The book applies to today's people much more than in the days when Joseph Smith translated it, because it speaks about the way it is now. I was traveling all over the world, and I saw many places, and I saw most of the prophecies being fulfilled; it's amazing. That really is a good book. There are many things in it that are coming true now. You just read the book and want to get baptized — and that's it."[17]

Summarizing his reasons for joining the Church, Cosic said, "There are a hundred reasons why I should not join the Church, and only one reason why I should — because it is true. I joined The Church of Jesus Christ of Latter-day Saints for one main reason, and that was because of the relationship I had developed with God personally."[18]

After his baptism, Kresimir continued to voraciously study the gospel. His coaches and teammates recalled that he was rarely

Photo KK Zadar

seen without a church book in his hands. Coach Watts recalled a time when the team was getting ready for a conference game. "While most of the players were tense," Watts said, "Cosic was studying The Discourses of Brigham Young."[19]

Cosic began sharing the gospel with people back home in Yugoslavia while touring with his national team prior to his senior season. When he returned to Provo nearly a month later than expected, Coach Potter asked what had delayed him. Cosic explained that he had invited the audience at one of the national team's games to watch the Church film "Man's Search for Happiness." Government officials promptly bugged his phone and confiscated his passport. During Kreso's senior season, Potter noticed his star player was often tired during practices. When asked by the coach why he was tired, Kreso explained that he had been staying up until three or four o'clock in the morning translating the Book of Mormon into Croatian.[20]

In spite of Cosic's fame and popularity in his homeland, his conversion to the Church and his visible example as a member were often unpopular. Cosic's devotion to the Church was derided at the time by Tempo, a prominent European sports publication, which wrote that "Kresimir's stay in the USA has made him a religious fanatic." When he was asked if his friends back home were surprised by his conversion to Mormonism, Cosic said, "You bet they were surprised. That's the last thing they thought was going to happen." Asked if his new religious beliefs affected how people viewed him, he said, "Almost everyone thinks I'm crazy anyway, so that's nothing new. As far as popularity goes, I just live my life normally and play because I have fun. Now people know I'm a Mormon; some of them don't think becoming a Mormon was too smart a thing to do—most of them don't—but they just have to take me that way, and that's it."[21]

Upon his initial arrival in Utah and learning what was

forbidden by the BYU honor code, Cosic had asked Coach Witbeck what Mormons at BYU did for fun. A few years after his conversion, Kreso was asked if his LDS beliefs had interfered with having fun. "I think that's really the best part, because you can really have much bigger fun," he said. "When we talk about sin; sin does not seem so bad the day you do it. Of course you have fun when you go to parties and that, but you have so many troubles afterwards. It's not worth it at all. And this gospel is really nice now and afterwards also.

"I really believe that living the gospel is fun, but it is hard. It's hard to really live it. It's not hard if you don't. You can be a member on paper with everyone and do some of the same things. It's not hard to play with the team if you can just sit on the bench, if you don't have to practice or anything. But if you've got to go all the time, then it's kind of difficult. But I don't think it's worthwhile to ask if there is any sacrifice. There's no sacrifice at all. You don't sacrifice anything when you invest five cents and receive a thousand dollars in return."[22]

As Kreso completed his career at BYU he was drafted by the Los Angeles Lakers of the NBA. He had previously been drafted after his junior season by the Portland Trailblazers, but surprised many by passing up an NBA career. He would once again be drafted by the Boston Celtics in 1976, but again declined the opportunity to play in the NBA. Kreso passed up a sizeable sum of money by declining the offers. His friend Truman Madsen explained, "The offers from the NBA teams that drafted him in different years were multi-million dollar offers."[23] Instead, Cosic opted to return to his homeland and play for his local team in Zadar for a salary of $250 a week.[24]

When asked why he would pass up the money and prestige of an NBA career, Kreso said, "Money is not the main thing. You try to live happily. If you can do it, you do. I try to live so that I feel good, and if I feel good, then I am living well."[25]

Current LDS Church President Thomas S. Monson also developed a friendship with the basketball star and offered his perspective on Kreso's career choice. "I think it was his love for his country, and the fact that he knew if he stayed with that basketball team in Yugoslavia, and they were adored by the public, and that would be a door-opener for the Church. I think he thought first of the Kingdom of God and the blessings of the gospel for his countrymen more so than he thought of Kresimir Cosic himself."[26]

Over the past few decades, thousands of BYU athletes have put their athletic careers on hold for two years to serve as full-time missionaries for the Church. Exhibiting that same spirit of sacrifice, Cosic chose to forgo an NBA career and millions of dollars in order to serve as a missionary in his homeland for the remainder of his life.

Before returning home at the age of 23, Cosic was set apart by Apostle Gordon B. Hinckley as a missionary and the presiding priesthood authority in Yugoslavia. Shortly after he returned to Zadar, Elder Paul Nibley, the son of his close friend Hugh Nibley, was sent across the Adriatic Sea to Zadar from the Italy North Mission. Elder Nibley and his missionary companion began proselytizing in Zadar along with Cosic.[27] At the age of 23 and just two years after he was baptized, Cosic was tasked with establishing the Church in a communist country. Kreso faithfully and masterfully fulfilled his calling, eventually organizing branches of the Church in Zadar, Belgrade and Zagreb.

Two of the earliest converts in Yugoslavia were Miso and Ankica Ostarcevic. One of Kreso's teammates, Miso had learned about the gospel from discussions with Kreso during the team's road trips. Miso gained a testimony of the gospel through those discussions, and his wife Ankica was then taught the gospel and gained a testimony of her own.

As Miso and Ankica were leaving a theater one night, they

Miso and Ankica Ostarcevic at the LDS Church's 40th anniversary celebration in June, 2012

Photo Ryan Mattson

were met by Kreso who informed them that he had received permission from the presiding priesthood authorities to baptize them.[28] Kreso was insistent that they not wait another day, telling them to make preparations for that night. There were no church buildings or baptismal fonts in the country and they did not want to attract the attention of the communist government authorities, so they were careful in choosing a location. After a failed initial attempt, the three ventured out again along the coast of the Adriatic Sea after midnight and finally found a suitable location for Miso and Ankica to be baptized. The couple would later become the first Yugoslavian couple sealed for eternity in the temple.[29]

In 1975, Cosic began an earnest effort to complete the task of translating the Book of Mormon into Croatian. Miso Ostarcevic remembers the process well. "What he did was he found the best translator, a former Catholic priest...and he was the finest translator, and he worked alongside of him," said Miso.[30] The process would take more than four years. In 1979 the Book of Mormon was first published in Croatian for use in missionary work in Yugoslavia, and that translation is still in use to this day.[31] Over the following decade, Cosic also assisted in translating the Doctrine and Covenants, the Pearl of Great Price and the temple ceremony into Croatian.

Kreso also continued his basketball career in Zadar, relishing the experience of playing for his home town team. "In Zadar when the crowd gets up, it's a crazy house," he said. "I have played all over the world, but I wouldn't change that crowd for any other. We've got 2,700 seats, and our place is just too small. Six thousand people try to squeeze in, so it's loud, and you can hear it. If 7:30 is game time, at 5:30 the house is full. It's so full that if you don't get there early, it's all over.

"I played on three championship teams in Zadar, and it was always a highlight, because when we win something over there, the whole town celebrates. Everyone dances; there is no work; everything closes. You can go outside, and you can see it's a completely different place for a week. Those are maybe the most impressive things. In the United States there is not so much celebration. In Zadar we have happiness. We have a good time winning the game."[32]

Kreso frequently used his basketball stardom as a means to introduce people to the gospel. Ankica Ostarcevic explained that everybody wanted BYU t-shirts, even though they didn't know what BYU meant, because Cosic wore them. She said Cosic would always bring a lot of the shirts with him and when kids asked for one, he would require them to learn the Articles of Faith in order to get one. Former BYU athletic trainer Marv Roberson told of a time when Kreso invited a group of basketball players from Zadar to a special meeting at the hotel where Roberson was staying during a team trip. When the players arrived, Cosic showed them a film of his basketball highlights and then followed it with the film "Man's Search for Happiness."[33]

In addition to the championships he won with his local team from Zadar, Cosic led the Yugoslavian national team to a gold medal in the 1978 World Championships, followed by a gold medal in the 1980 Olympic Games. Cosic ended his career as the nation's all-time scoring leader and would forever be considered a sports and cultural icon in the former Yugoslavia.

His fame and popularity also made Kreso the ideal person to establish the Church in his homeland. "His influence was the type of influence we could get in no other way, from no other person with the same talents," President Monson said. "I give him the credit for being a magic key in the Lord's hand to open Yugoslavia so those people could hear the gospel of Jesus Christ."[34] In October 1985, Monson, then a member of the Quorum of the Twelve, dedicated Yugoslavia for missionary work. During the same trip, Elder Monson dedicated the

Church's meeting house in Zagreb, with his friend Kresimir serving as translator for both dedication ceremonies.

In 1980, a friend introduced Kreso to a French professor living in Zagreb by the name of Ljerka Kobasic. They married in 1982 and had three children: Ana, Eva and Kresimir Junior. Ana would eventually follow in her father's footsteps by playing basketball for BYU. In 1983 Kresimir was honored by his alma mater as an inductee into the BYU Athletic Hall of Fame.

Cosic had loyal followings in both Provo and his home country, but his fame went far beyond those locales. Kreso played professionally in Italy from 1978 to 1980 and his basketball fame extended throughout Europe. Former teammate Vlado Vanjak recalled an experience after their playing careers had ended. Vlado and Kreso went to watch a basketball game together in Bologna, Italy. They arrived after the game had started, hoping to sneak in unnoticed. "As soon as everyone realized that he had come into the stadium, they stopped the basketball game and everyone in the audience gave him a ten minute standing ovation," Vanjak recalled. "I have goose bumps just thinking about it because I've never seen a basketball game stopped so that the athletes and everyone could give someone a standing ovation."[35]

After retiring as a player, Cosic became the coach of the Yugoslavian national team from 1985 to 1987. During this time, he coached and developed some of the greatest players the country ever produced, including Drazen Petrovic, Toni Kukoc, Dino Radja and Vlade Divac. All four players were members of the 1987 European championship team coached by Cosic, a team that then won a silver medal at the Seoul Olympics in 1988. Kreso's four protégés were then drafted in the NBA, where they began a new wave of European NBA stars, forever changing the makeup of the world's top professional league.

On March 31, 1991 Croatia declared its independence from the

Socialist Federal Republic of Yugoslavia, beginning a war with the Serbian-controlled Yugoslav People's Army that would last until 1995. Hoping to bring an end to the war and to improve the knowledge of Croatia in the outside world, Cosic accepted a request to serve as the deputy Croatian Ambassador to the United States. "The President (of Croatia) thought Washington was the most important city to us after our capital of Zagreb," Cosic explained at the time. "He sent me here because I know America."[36]

Kreso became the face of Croatia for many in the United States government, but considered working in politics a much easier job than coaching basketball. "Politics is actually not so hard," he said. "Being a coach is much harder. If anything goes wrong, you are wrong. Anything," he said with a grin, adding that even if a player was injured in a game or hurt in a car accident, it is always the coach's fault.

"In politics, whatever you do wrong, there is always somebody else to be blamed," Cosic explained. "So it gets very, you know, simple. I just don't like it. I think that's one of the things I brought to politics. I've learned in my life to take the blame for what I did and sometimes for others. In politics it's just different. It's not so much a question of knowledge. You get seasoned. Being a coach, for example, in the former Yugoslavia and Italy and Greece, you've really got to understand politics. You've got to understand it much better than politicians do if you want to be that."[37]

Kresimir was finally able to leave politics when the Croatian War of Independence ended in 1995. Kreso missed coaching during the war and was hoping to return to his former profession. However, he would not have that opportunity. During a routine physical in 1994, Kreso's doctor found a small nodule on his neck. While the doctor wasn't overly concerned with what he saw, Cosic was. He called Barney Madsen, the son of Truman and

Ann, who was nearby at the time. "'Barney, I need you to come and give me a blessing,'" Truman recalled Cosic saying. "'I've just talked to the doctor, and where I'm going I won't need a suitcase.' And that's his typical irony."[38] Cosic was soon diagnosed with non-Hodgkin's lymphoma and began treatments.

In an interview with the Deseret News at the time, Cosic said he still hoped to get back into coaching basketball someday, but wasn't sure that would be possible because of the cancer. "It is what I would like to do, not necessarily what I will do. You never know what will happen. My country may need me to do something more. Or maybe God will have other ideas."[39]

Kreso began treatment in Baltimore, Maryland and the initial prognosis was good. He responded well to treatments and was soon told that he was cancer-free. Hoping to avoid a recurrence of the cancer, Cosic opted to also undergo a bone marrow transplant. Unfortunately, his liver was weak as a result of a bout with Hepatitis. His body was unable to withstand the bone marrow transplant and it soon became clear to Kreso and his loved ones that death was imminent.

During his final days, Cosic was visited by his dear friend Hugh Nibley. "He was just really very sick," Phyllis Nibley recalled. "He was in the hospital bed. When we got there and he saw us he tried to sit up. He was just filled with joy to see my husband. He had wanted so much to talk to him and my husband spent two or three hours with him the next two days and then he slipped into a coma."[40]

Truman and Ann Madsen were also with Cosic in his final days. "The last time he prayed and the next-to-last time he prayed, he prayed that the Lord would bless those who had been fasting and praying for him that they would not have their faith shaken when he went," Ann remembered. "And after he said that, the last time he said it, I said, 'Kreso, you don't need to worry about our family. We'll be OK.'"[41]

As she came to the realization that she was about to lose her beloved husband after just 13 years of marriage, Ljerka was deeply saddened. In addition to her own personal loss, Ljerka lamented that their three children would grow up without their father being a part of their lives. On May 25, 1995, Kresimir Cosic passed away at the age of 46. As his family and friends mourned his passing, so did the entire nation of Croatia which had lost one of its national heroes. On the day he died, a basketball game was being played in Belgrade, Serbia. Although Kreso was a Croat, the Serbian fans' love for him superseded the animosity that had resulted from the war between the two nations. When it was announced that Cosic had passed away, the 20,000 people in attendance stood up and observed a moment of silence in honor of Cosic.

Fra Bonaventura Duda, a Catholic priest from Zadar, spoke at Kreso's funeral. "Our Kreso, ever since I have known him, was a faithful believer, but he did not (merely) speak of it, he performed his faith. He did not only believe in this religion, he truly believed in a personal connection with God. He wholeheartedly tried to practice his faith in real life. Thank you, oh God, for having created Kreso and made him of such good nature."[42] Cosic was buried in the Mirogoj cemetery in Zagreb, Crotia, only a few feet from the grave of Drazen Petrovic.[43] Petrovic, the Croatian basketball phenom who had been coached by Cosic before becoming an NBA star, died at the age of 28 in a tragic car accident in 1993.

Since his passing, Kreso received numerous posthumous honors in Croatia and beyond. Local officials in Zagreb honored Kreso by naming a public square located next to the nation's sports complex in his honor. His hometown of Zadar also honored its favorite son, bestowing the name Kresimir Cosic Hall on its new sports arena. At the time of its completion in 2008, it was the largest sports arena in Croatia. Fittingly, a towering 15-

Kresimir Cosic Hall in Zadar, Croatia   Photo Andrej Salov

Kresimir Cosic Hall (interior)   Photo Veliki Meshtar

foot statue of Cosic stands outside.

Commenting during the 2005 NCAA basketball tournament on the influx of international talent into American basketball, legendary CBS basketball analyst Billy Packer called Cosic "the first great international player to play college basketball in the United States."[44]

BYU head basketball coach Dave Rose also witnessed the fame and impact of Cosic while his Cougars were playing in Europe one summer. "When we toured Europe a couple of summers ago, everywhere we went, they knew BYU basketball because of Cosic," Rose said.[45]

On May 7, 1996, Cosic was inducted into the Basketball Hall of Fame in Springfield, Massachusetts along with NBA stars George Gervin, David Thompson and Gail Goodrich, and women's basketball pioneer Nancy Lieberman-Cline. Kreso was also inducted into the Utah Basketball Hall of Fame in 2001 and the FIBA Hall of Fame in 2007.

Brigham Young University officially retired Cosic's number 11 jersey in a ceremony at the Marriott Center on March 4, 2006. Cosic and Danny Ainge are the only men's basketball players to have received that honor from BYU.

Even after his passing, Cosic was able to fill the Marriott Center one last time. "He not only remained a really gifted athlete but ... he became a better man and became quite a tribute to his family, to his land, and to his religion," said Steve Kelly, a former BYU teammate.[46]

Ljerka and her children traveled from Croatia to the United States to attend the ceremony and were visibly touched by the experience. "It is very impressive that Kreso is not forgotten here," said daughter Ana amidst the cheers from the capacity crowd. "Kreso never forgot Provo. I don't think he ever really left it."

LDS Church building in Zadar   Photo Ryan Mattson

Ljerka Cosic accepts an award from Danko Radic, President of the Croatian
Basketball Federation in 2008

Photo Robert Valai/Getty

Ljerka was also moved by the outpouring of love for her husband. "I am touched to see that they honor him here so far away from his country and seeing that he is not forgotten," she wrote in a statement that was read by Ana.[47]

NOTES AND SOURCES

CHAPTER 2: CURTIS BROWN
1. Brown, C. (2004, February 24). Curtis Brown baptism testimony of faith for family. Total Blue Sports. Retrieved from http://byu.scout.com/2/236859.html.

CHAPTER 4 - CORBY EASON:
1. Feinauer, J. (2011, August 17). Rise up with Corby Eason [television broadcast]. In True Blue. Provo, UT: BYU Athletic Communications.
2. Ibid.
3. Ibid.
4. Ibid.
5. Harmon, D. (2012, July 30). Former BYU defensive back Corby Eason has high expectations for 2012 Cougars. The Deseret News. Retrieved from http://www.deseretnews.com/article/765593406/Former-BYU-defensive-back-Corby-Eason-has-high-expectations-for-2012-Cougars.html?pg=all.
6. Feinauer, J.
7. Gurney, B. (2011, December 24). Eason has thrived in BYU's unique environment. The Deseret News. Retrieved from http://www.deseretnews.com/article/700209917/BYU-football-Eason-has-thrived-in-BYUs-unique-environment.html?pg=all.
8. Ibid.

CHAPTER 8 – SHAUN NUA:
1. Strasemeier, S. (2012, January 26). Shaun Nua Named Assistant Football Coach At The Naval Academy. Navy Sports. Retrieved from http://www.navysports.com/sports/m-footbl/spec-rel/012612aaa.html.

CHAPTER 9 – KRESIMIR COSIC:

1. Jurdana, L. (2007, November 29). An off-court story: The life of Kresimir Cosic [documentary film]. Provo, UT: Brigham Young University Department of Communications.

2. Rock, B. (2006, March 4). Mission: Possible for Cosic. The Deseret News. Retrieved from http://www.deseretnews.com/article/635189424/Mission-Possible--for-Cosic.html?pg=all.

3. Ibid.

4. Ibid.

5. Jurdana

6. Ibid.

7. Harmon, D. (2006, March 2). Late Cougar Cosic's talent, fun couldn't be contained. The Deseret News. Retrieved from http://www.deseretnews.com/article/635188744/Late-Cougar-Cosics-talent-fun-couldnt-be-contained.html?pg=all.

8. Putnam, P. (1973, January 22). The Week. Sports Illustrated. Retrieved from http://sportsillustrated.cnn.com/vault/article/magazine/MAG1086970/3/index.htm.

9. Jurdana

10. Ibid.

11. Pacrac, T. (2011, October 3). Ahead of his time. SLAM Magazine. Retrieved from: http://www.slamonline.com/online/the-magazine/features/2011/10/ahead-of-his-time-kresimir-cosic/.

12. Stahle, S. (2006, January 21) National hero: Town square named in Kresimir Cosic's honor. The Church News. Retrieved from http://www.ldschurchnews.com/articles/48423/National-hero.html.

13. Ibid.

14. Jurdana

15. Davis & Hiatt

16. Stahle

17. Davis, D. & Hiatt, D. (1974, February) Kresimir Cosic – basketball

and baptism. The New Era. Retrieved from https://www.lds.org/new-era/1974/02/kresimir-cosic-basketball-and-baptism?lang=eng.

18. Stahle

19. Ibid.

20. Harmon

21. Davis & Hiatt

22. Ibid.

23. Jurdana

24. Rothlisberger, J. (2006, March 4) Cosic jersey retired. BYU Athletic Communications. Retrieved from http://byucougars.com/m-basketball/cosic-jersey-retired.

25. Davis & Hiatt

26. Jurdana

27. Hundric, A. (2008, December) History of the Church in Croatia. Retrieved from http://www.crkvaisusakrista.hr/fileadmin/_temp_/History.pdf.

28. Stahle

29. Hundric

30. Jurdana

31. Hundric

32. Davis & Hiatt

33. Jurdana

34. Ibid.

35. Ibid.

36. Stahle

37. Jurdana

38. Ibid.

39. Harmon

40. Jurdana

41. Ibid.

42. Stahle

43. Stankovic, V. (2011, November 26). Kresimir Cosic, A player ahead of his time. Euroleague Basketball. Retrieved from

http://www.euroleague.net/features/voices/2011-2012/vladimir-stankovic/i/90320/6180/kresimir-cosic-a-player-ahead-of-his-time.

44. Stahle

45. Harmon

46. Bluth, T. (2006, March 6). Former BYU All-American's Jersey Retired. BYU Daily Universe. Retrieved from http://nn.byu.edu/story.cfm/58751.

47. Call, J. (2006, March 5). BYU retires Cosic's No. 11 jersey. The Deseret News. Retrieved from http://www.deseretnews.com/article/635189523/BYU-retires-Cosics-No-11-jersey.html?pg=all.

59062419R00093

Made in the USA
Middletown, DE
09 August 2019